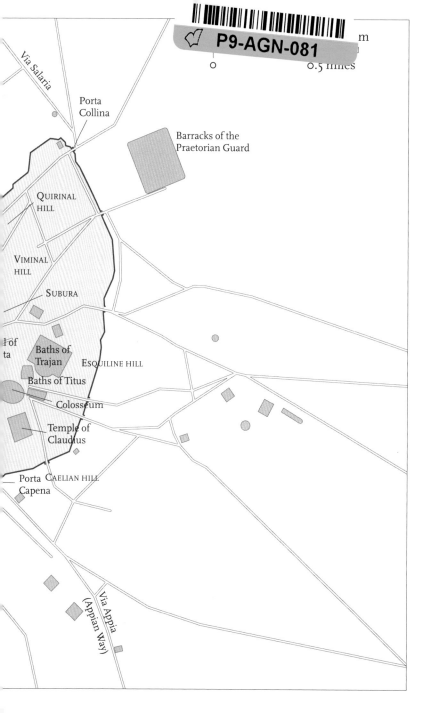

m

0   0.5 miles

Via Salaria

Porta
Collina

Barracks of the
Praetorian Guard

QUIRINAL
HILL

VIMINAL
HILL

SUBURA

l of
ta

Baths of
Trajan

ESQUILINE HILL

Baths of Titus

Colosseum

Temple of
Claudius

Porta   CAELIAN HILL
Capena

Via Appia
(Appian Way)

JUAN CARLOS SIERRA PALACIOS

MEMORIAL COLLECTION

BELOVED FATHER, HUSBAND, & SON
COLLECTOR OF BOOKS, TOYS, & MOVIES

10 marzo 1977 - 30 diciembre 2020

CAVE CANEM

CAVE CANEM

A MISCELLANY OF LATIN WORDS & PHRASES

LORNA ROBINSON

METRO BOOKS
New York

METRO BOOKS
New York

An Imprint of Sterling Publishing
387 Park Avenue South
New York, NY 10016

© 2008 by Elwin Street Productions
Conceived and produced by
Elwin Street Productions
3 Percy Street
London, W1T 1DE
United Kingdom
www.elwinstreet.com

ISBN 978-1-4351-5425-4

For information about custom editions, special sales, and premium and
corporate purchases, please contact Sterling Special Sales at 800-805-5489 or
specialsales@sterlingpublishing.com.

Manufactured in Singapore

2 4 6 8 10 9 7 5 3 1

www.sterlingpublishing.com

CONTENTS

TIMELINE OF THE CITY OF ROME

BCE

753	Foundation of Rome
753–509	Rome as a Kingdom; the rule of the kings, ending with Tarquinius Superbus
509	Expulsion of the Kings; start of the Republic
450	First law code: the Twelve Tables
390	Rome sacked by Gauls
378	Rome's city wall built
312	Appian Way built
287	End of struggle between patricians and plebeians; some laws for equal rights
272	Rome wins control of whole of Italy
264–241	First Punic War (against Carthage)
264	First gladiatorial games
218–201	Second Punic War: Hannibal defeated
214–167	Macedonian Wars; comedies of Plautus and Terence; poetry of Ennius
149–146	Third Punic War: Carthage destroyed
91–87	Roman citizenship extended to all Italy
82–81	Dictatorship of Sulla; rise of Pompey
63	Consulship of Cicero; conspiracy of Catiline
60	"First triumvirate" (Pompey, Julius Caesar, Crassus)
58–50	Julius Caesar conquers Gaul; expeditions to Britain
49–45	Julius Caesar wins civil war against Pompey
44	Julius Caesar dictator for life; assassinated March 15th (the Ides of March)
43	"Second triumvirate" (Antony, Octavian, Lepidus); murder of Cicero
32–31	Octavian wins civil war against Mark Antony
29	Virgil's *Georgics*

27	Start of the empire; Octavian becomes first emperor Augustus
19	Virgil's *Aeneid*; poetry of Horace and Ovid
CE	
14	Death of Augustus; succeeded by Tiberius
69	Year of the four emperors: Galba, Otho, Vitellius, and Vespasian
69–79	Rule of Vespasian; histories of Pliny the Elder
79	Eruption of Vesuvius
81–96	Rule of Domitian; epigrams of Martial, letters of Pliny the Younger, satires of Juvenal
96–180	The rules of Nerva, Trajan, Hadrian, Antoninus Pius, and Marcus Aurelius
122	Biographies of Suetonius
212	Roman citizenship extended to all free inhabitants of the empire
234–284	Crisis of the Third Century; political anarchy
284–305	Rule of Diocletian; Roman Empire split in two, Diocletian ruling the East, Maximian the West
376–382	First war against the Visigoths
379–395	Rule of Theodosius; Rome politically unified for the final time
406	Germanic tribes succeed in crossing the Rhine
408	Western legions disintegrate following the execution of army general, Stilicho
410	Sack of Rome by the Visigoths; first time in 800 years that Rome falls to a foreign enemy
455	Sack of Rome by the Vandals
461–468	Failed counterstrikes against the Vandals
476	Deposition of the last western emperors; loss of western Roman Empire complete

IMPORTO

The history of Latin is an incredible survival story. It is that of a living, constantly evolving, and immensely influential language, which has survived all these centuries and connects deeply and powerfully to our modern world. Latin itself, an old Italic language that derived from ancient Greek, first arrived to the site of Rome with migrating Latin people around the ninth century BCE. There on the banks of the river Tiber it settled, and quietly but steadily the seed of this language grew within this once tiny and unknown community. It spread and thrived, and eventually it became an essential part of the might and fame of the Roman Empire. The Romans excelled at conquest, and they took their language with them wherever they went across the world.

At its heyday ancient Rome would have been much like a bustling modern city. People from all corners of its rapidly expanding empire flooded its labyrinthine streets, which were lined with tall unwieldy-looking tower blocks, *insulae*, where huge families were crammed into tiny living spaces. Shops, *tabernae*, and vendors, *tabernarii*, also filled the streets, with their goods spilling out onto the streets just like the grocers, food stands, and silk stores I walk past in the city streets each day; a warren of shops filled with a seething crowd of people. You would have found an old Greek man bickering over prices with a North African, while a Roman schoolboy hurried home past a Spanish tradesman. All walks of life, all races and religions lived and worked side by side, in a place where we're told the curse of insomnia and the early morning bustle kept the writer Pliny awake. It was a place of life and diversity, not the motionless, grand, lonely place suggested by the vast stone skeletons of mighty buildings and the dusty grammar books that remain for us today.

While the grandeur of Rome eventually deteriorated, and its dominion receded, the Latin language defiantly prospered, laying down strong, enduring roots, which later grew into the various Romance languages. Alongside this, as the Roman Catholic Church grew in power and influence, it adopted Latin as its ecclesiastical language, which furthered its lasting influence. Today, in medical, legal, scientific, and many other fields, you cannot escape the impact and prevalence of Latin.

This book will give you a taste of the wonderful, chimeric world of ancient Rome and its language. Each chapter explores a different aspect of daily life in ancient Rome, and looks at the words and concepts that have shaped our language and culture today; and it doesn't just look at the lives of the very rich, but at the kind of world that most people would have known as well, with a peek at the underbelly of Roman life that can so easily be forgotten.

lares familiares
"household gods"
ab ovo ad mala
"from the egg to the apples"

UBI BENE IBI DOMUS

"where it's good, there's home"

The houses of different cultures, countries, and communities diverge enormously, and their differences—where they place their rooms, what rooms they have—tell us so much about the outlook of a people and the ways in which their communities function on a daily basis.

This particular phrase was originally coined by the Roman tragic poet Pacuvius. For the ancient Romans, the home was an important base, a place of comfort and security, and also a place to entertain, to decorate and express themselves. There were many different types of places to live, each of which expressed a person's status, hopes, beliefs, and way of life. From the large private house known as the *domus*, to the *insulae*, flimsy fire-prone, high-rise apartments which grew taller and taller as necessity demanded, there were homes of all kinds in the city of Rome, and each one told a complex and colorful tale.

It has often been said that the Romans were a much more social people than we are today, and their homes were designed very much with this in mind. From rich to very poor, the houses and apartments reveal what their owners' domestic lives were like: what the Romans used the rooms for and what their routines were.

janus
[*ya*-nus]
god of doorways and beginnings

It is appropriate to start with Janus, the Roman god of doorways and beginnings. A god with two faces, one facing forward and one back, he took his name from *ianua*, "door," and then gave it to January, the first month of the year.

Unusually for a Roman god, he had no real counterpart in ancient Greek mythology. He watched over passageways into buildings, and was said to be both just outside and just inside of a home. Janus, as with so many of the Roman gods, also had a taste for chasing nymphs, for according to Roman myth he used his double-sided vision to win over the nymph Carna. He gave her power over door hinges, and her name was then changed to Cardea, which comes from *cardo* meaning a hinge. It seems a strange gift, but the Romans were very careful to worship spirits attached to even the most minute things to ensure the smooth running of their lives. It certainly adds a new dimension to the creaking of hinges around the house.

Janus was one of the important household gods, and families would be sure to pray to him and leave him sacrificial gifts at significant events such as births, marriages, and harvests. And every time they passed into their homes, they spared a thought for the god lingering at the threshold.

domus
[*do*-mus]
home

This was the name for the private home of a well-off Roman. Giving us various words like "domestic" and "domicile," it was the abode of the wealthy middle and upper classes, a one-story building with multiple rooms and an enclosed garden. One of the most startling things about these homes was the blind face they turned towards the outside world. Glass would have been expensive and difficult to source, so the walls that faced the street were stern and windowless to protect their occupants from the noise and smells of the city roads. It gave the occupants a feeling of being sealed off from the world in a sort of retreat, since once inside the bustle of the city was nearly nonexistent. The exteriors often had graffiti scrawled across them. While this is not something we tolerate, perhaps in the self-sealed, unseeing silence created by their thick walls, the owners did not regard this as a problem, instead seeing the outward face of these walls as public property.

vestibulum
[wes-*ti*-bul-um]
forecourt

Our modern word "vestibule" means a small area between an inner and outer door, or in medical terminology, a chamber such as in our ears.

The *vestibulum* in ancient Rome was slightly different. Houses in the city were built right on the street, and the distance

Bene lava ("wash [your feet] well!"), a mosaic from the entrance to a Roman villa.

between the street and entrance said a lot about one's status in society. The houses of the poor opened straight out onto the bustling paths of the city, with no grand entrance or exit to speak of. On opening their front door, they would find themselves unceremoniously deposited into the bright sunlight and chaos of a city street. The tiny gap between the door threshold and the street was their *vestibulum*.

But the wealthy *domus* owner, on the other hand, had a passage leading up to the entrance, usually through shops; this passageway was called the *vestibulum*. It was a sort of courtyard area, and would often be decorated like a garden with flowers, plants, and other similar ornamentations. In the early morning a group of visitors known as *clientes* would gather here daily, awaiting their entrance to the house of their patron, who would then duly hand out *sportula*, which were little baskets of rations and money.

The Roman satirist Juvenal remarked cynically on the tradition: "Look now at the meager dole set down upon the threshold for a toga-clad mob to scramble for! Yet the patron first peers into your face, fearing that you may be claiming under someone else's name: once recognized, you will get your share." This custom might sound like an ancient version of a welfare line, complete with weary officials scanning records with a suspicious eye, but these clients were expected to offer favors in return for their gift baskets.

ianitor
[*yan*-it-or]
doorkeeper

In the *ostium* (entrance) of the Roman *domus*, one might have found a phrase or word over the door, such as *salve*, "greetings." One might also have encountered a tough-looking slave standing just inside the door, watching anyone who came to the doorway with a sharp gaze. This slave had the role of the doorkeeper, *ianitor*, a word that has stayed with us through the ages and is still very much in use today, except the "i" has become a "j" to give us "janitor."

The Roman writer Ovid wrote a poem to one such doorkeeper who had refused to let the drunken, lovesick poet in to see his mistress. He started off with a string of wheedles, "Look—you can see, then, undo the lock—the doorway's wet with my tears!" before descending into downright abuse, and finally staggering off into the early hours in his debauched stupor.

fauces
[*fow*-kays]
jaws

The name for the whole entrance area, from the *vestibulum* through to the *ianua*, it meant the "jaws" of the house, which is a striking and threatening association. "The jaws of Hell" was, and still is, a common image, and may have had a particular resonance for ancient visitors entering the homes of others—

Virgil used the word to describe the entrance to the underworld in his famous epic, the *Aeneid*.

A curtain, *velum*, separated this entrance from the inside of the house. The visitor would have to draw this back in order to step into the inner sanctum of the *domus*. Perhaps this added to the feel of entering either an urban retreat or a shadowy other world; one passed through the thick, blind walls, past the doorman, and finally through the curtain into the mysterious room on the other side.

cave canem
[*ka*-weh *kan*-em]
beware of the dog

As if the mighty stone jaws of the Roman *domus* weren't enough, there was sometimes another literal set of jaws awaiting the unwary visitor, in the form of a dog chained inside the *fauces*. This set up may remind one of the entrance to the Roman underworld, guarded, it was said, by a three-headed dog called Cerberus. In fact, it seems likely that some owners would have found a certain ironic amusement in naming their pet dog

cave canem, "beware of dog," a Roman mosaic.

after this creature. The family dog was often accompanied by the inscription, *cave canem*. Dogs were common pets in Roman homes and popular with children who liked to play games with their domestic animals, as they still do today.

impluvium
[im-*plu*-wi-um]
rainwater pool

One of the first things one would have noticed in a Roman home was a conspicuous hole in the roof known as the *compluvium*— from *pluit* "it rains" and the prefix *con* "together." This hole was there by design, and through it fell the gentle sunlight of March, the brilliant rays of summer, and also, of course, the

Mosaic of a fish from a Roman Amphitheater, from 1st century BCE.

rain. It allowed air in the rooms to circulate in times of baking heat. The rainwater was collected in a shallow pool beneath the *compluvium*, which was known as the *impluvium*, and formed a pleasant centerpiece to the house. There were often beautiful mosaic effects around the pool, such as a fish relief shimmering through the shallow water.

atrium
[*a*-tri-um]
hall

The *atrium* of a Roman house was very much the centerpiece of the home, where people passed through and the breeze circulated and pumped into the connecting rooms. It was a public part of the house, hence its peculiarly hybrid status; being somewhere between a room and a courtyard, it was open to the elements.

An *atrium* today is a grand reception area, often with a high roof or glass ceiling. The word may be more familiar from biology since its plural *atria* are otherwise known as the upper chambers of the heart.

imagines
[im-*a*-gin-ays]
portraits

This is the plural of *imago*, which has come straight into our language in the form of words like "images," "imagination," and "imaginary." *Imagines* were portraits of noble ancestors, and they would have been found all around the *atrium*, along with other grand busts and statues. They would have been placed there for the owners' own appreciation and delectation, but also, and more importantly, to demonstrate to visitors information about their social standing.

Would-be philosophers would have busts of their gurus on display, and literary types would have bookcases filled with appropriate material. Decorations like this were in abundance in the *atrium* since this was the main socializing venue of the house. The always-scathing Juvenal wrote about unlearned people who would keep "their houses crammed with plaster casts of Chrysippus," a Greek philosopher and a most noble ancestor indeed.

Lares Familiares
[*lah*-rays fa-mil-i-*ah*-rays]
household gods

The *Lares Familiares* were a set of household deities, the spirits that protected people's homes, and legend has it that they were the children of Mercury and Lara. This union supposedly occurred as a result of Lara having her tongue cut off for telling secrets about Jupiter's philandering; Mercury was then ordered to escort her to the gates of the underworld, but he fell in love with her on the way, the inevitable happened, and thence came two children, the *Lares*. As time went by, these *Lares* became confused with a profusion of gods and spirits that hung about the house and other places, so it's fair to say that by Augustus' time, in late 1st century BCE, no one had much of a clue who or what they were worshipping exactly, but they continued to do so anyway. They worshipped at a shrine on one wall, with snakes and leaves around it, and a little niche for offerings. It was called the *lararium*, and the family would give gifts, burn incense, and say prayers to the *Lares*, in the hope that this would keep their homes and livelihoods safe.

triclinium
[tri-*klin*-i-um]
dining room

At the far corner of the *atrium*, was one of the most important rooms of the Roman house, the dining room.

Its name means "three couches" (from the ancient Greek *tres* and *klinai*) and refers to the Roman custom of taking meals lying down, which might now seem a bit ill-

Roman mosaic depicting a slave bringing the requisites of a banquet. 3rd century CE, Carthage.

conceived to those who dislike indigestion and mild nausea during dinner. However, Roman men saw it as a mark of their civilized nature to take their meals reclining on a couch, as the position represented a relaxed social demeanor. Women, children, and slaves would eat in the far more uncivilized manner of sitting at a table, in a chair with a back known as a *cathedra*.

Three couches or *lecti* were arranged in the *triclinium*; men would lie on them, propped up by their left elbow, so their right arm was free to use. From the descriptions of ancient writers, it seems that up to four men would recline on one couch, and in a distinct order defined by their rank. Each individual would have been acutely aware of his place in the hierarchy.

The dinner party was a central part of Roman life. It would start in the late afternoon and stretch into the night, as the food would be followed by music, poetry, and conversation. For this reason, in some wealthy houses there were as many as four *triclinia* positioned around the house to make best use of the shade in the summer heat or the winter sun in chillier times.

The food often consisted of a series of elaborate and sometimes bizarre dishes, which paraded the host's wealth—perhaps even at the expense of pleasing the tastebuds and nourishing the body. We read of men eating seven-course meals and Juvenal referred to people who went to the baths with "undigested peacock" in their stomachs and consequently died.

One might have found, among the many decorations in the *triclinium*, a mosaic of a scene from the *Aeneid*, plants, or grand statues of famous mythical characters. This room, like the *atrium*, was designed to impress.

ab ovo ad mala
[ab o-vo ad *mal*-a]
from the egg to the apples

This expression was coined by the Roman poet Horace and
it literally means "from the egg to the apples," describing the
beginning and end of a typical Roman meal. It was customary
to begin with an egg course and end with some fruit, and he
was using the metaphor of the Roman dinner to describe a full
and complete process.

These days, we still sometimes use this phrase to indicate
something that's done thoroughly and completely; there's also
a shortened version of it very much in currency, *ab ovo*, which is
used to mean "from the beginning."

pisces natare oportet
[*pis*-kays na-*tah*-reh o-*por*-tet]
fish need to swim

The Roman writer Petronius first used this expression to
encourage someone to drink up the wine at a meal. As well as
the care taken with the numerous dishes sometimes served up
at the Roman *cena*, "dinner," what one drank with these courses
was also important.

Wine was very important to the Romans, it was their strongest
drink. Pliny the Elder wrote about the various processes of
production, and lamented the decline of good vintages. The
wine would have been mixed with water for drinking, and

sometimes salt water might even have been added. While the Greeks used wine more for stimulating conversation and gently loosening inhibitions, the Romans had more of a tendency to get staggeringly drunk. Obviously the fish didn't just need to swim, but to have a whole ocean within which to do it.

The phrase has since become a well-known adage used to mean "people act according to their nature," although notably in Scotland, Petronius' original meaning has been preserved.

peristylium
[per-is-*stil*-i-um]
a courtyard surrounded by columns

This word comes straight from the ancient Greek and meant a court, or *stylium*, surrounded by columns, or *peri*. Ancient Greek houses had an "inner" garden, inside the house, and the Romans took this idea and made it their own. This garden became an absolutely central part of the Roman house. We still occasionally use the word "peristyle" today, and the cloister was an architectural feature that developed from the *peristylium*.

The *peristylium* was a lovely refreshing feature of the home. It was filled with colorful, exotic plants and flowers, and occasionally statues, ponds (*piscinae*, raising fish, could actually be a very fruitful business enterprise), and fountain features. The Romans loved their city and its bustling urban ways—but the prevalence of these gardens incorporated into the center of houses tells also of their love of nature. Roses, mulberry and fig trees, marigolds, narcissi, violets, hyacinths, saffron, cassia, cypress, and thyme are all examples of the kinds of plants one might have found in the garden of a *domus*. Typically the *peristylium* was in the private area of the house; however, some wealthy Romans went so far as to have two gardens, one public and one private.

barba Iovis
[*bar*-ba *yo*-wis]
beard of Jupiter

If one looked closely at the flower bed of a Roman *peristylium*, one might well have seen a plant that looks like a collection of green roses. It's called a *sempervivum*—from the Latin *semper* "always" and *vivum* "living"—referring to its stubbornly resistant nature, as it is able to survive in most conditions, from the heat of summer to the frosts of winter. We know the plant today as "hen and chicks," a type of succulent. Many Romans had them in their gardens and on their rooftops. They thought that these plants were special to the ruler of the gods, Jupiter, and they called the plant *barba Iovis*, "beard of Jupiter," because they believed that his beard could be seen in the flowers.

Even more unlikely was the superstition that these plants protected against your home being struck by lightning (Jupiter was the god of the thunderbolt). Recently people have observed that there may be a grain of truth in this theory as the pointed-shaped leaves may mean that the equalization of the electrical charge between the house and the air is eased, and so there is less chance of a spark discharge.

culina
[ku-*lin*-a]
kitchen

Giving us our word "culinary," this is the Romans' word for the kitchen. As in our homes, the kitchen was an important room for obvious reasons. It was the domain of the slave, and particularly of the *coquus*, the cook of the house, upon whose shoulders rested the task of feeding both the family and its guests, as well as making sure the slaves were not going about their tasks with rumbling stomachs and expressions of hunger. The Roman kitchen was typically cramped and small. There was a primitive oven for cooking, and a work surface, but not a great deal more.

dum meus adsiduo luceat igne focus
[dum-*me*-us ad-*sid*-oo-oh loo-*ke*-at *ig*-neh *foh*-kus]
while my hearth gleams with a constant flame

These words, from the war-shy and home-loving Roman poet Tibullus, remind us of one of the most important features of a Roman home—that is, the *focus* or "hearth." It gives us our words "focus" and "focal," for things that are the center of our attention, as the fire, the source of warmth (and cooked food in poorer dwellings that would not have had a separate kitchen), was very much the symbolic center of the ancient house. In earlier times it used to be found in the *atrium*, but no one is quite sure where it then moved to. It was kept constantly burning, as the quote suggests, and in the absence of smoke alarms, the fire brigade, which usually consisted of a gang of slaves, was frequently called on.

cubiculum
[ku-*bi*-ku-lum]
bedroom

This word comes into English as a "cubicle," a small room, such as a changing room in a clothes shop, characterized by its minimal box-shape. Originally, this was the name for a Roman

Birds depicted in a mosaic floor, from Pompeii.

bedroom, and in fact this is a pretty apt description of what the Roman bedroom was like. There was not a lot in it, other than a bed, *lectus*. Sometimes the remains of a floor shows us clearly where the bed would have stood, indicated by a change in the mosaic pattern that would have covered the bedroom floor. The minimal nature of their bedrooms reflects the limited amount of time they spent there. Among the poor, married couples would share the same bed by necessity, but it seems that for wealthier Romans, the preferred arrangement was for the man and woman to sleep in separate beds and even separate bedrooms.

omina noctis
[*om*-in-uh *nok*-tis]
omens of the night

This haunting phrase gives us our words "omen" and "ominous," and of course "nocturnal" and "night." We may think of many things as we are emerging from the groggy depths of our dreams, but very few of us today would examine them for possible omens sent by the gods. The poet Tibullus reminds us that this was a common behavior for a Roman waking up at dawn, commenting that "the human race is doomed to worry." In a world governed in minute detail by all manner of deities who at any moment might have had needs to cater for or messages to send, the ancient Romans had to be constantly on their guard for clues and hints, and the mysterious nature of dreams meant they were prime candidates for superstitious habits and fears.

oleum et operam perdidi
[*o*-le-um et *op*-er-am per-*di*-di]
I've wasted oil and toil

Plautus, the Roman comic playwright, has one of his young women exclaim this in his play *Poenulus*, and it's an expression to describe a process that has been long and arduous and borne no fruit. The play was referring to the use of beauty products that were so much a part of the Roman woman's day. Rich Romans did not undress much for bed—the man only removed his toga and the woman would also sleep in her clothing, taking off only her outer garments, in her case a *stola*, an ankle length dress which indicated to the world that she was married.

Each morning, she would then set about beautifying her face and hair, laying out an array of trinkets and potions before her in all manner of tiny pots and vases, and with the help of an *ancilla*, "slave girl," would paint and dip and pad, applying the painstaking care of an artist, to achieve the look she wanted.

She would use *focus,* "ocher," to redden her lips and her cheeks, and *fuligo,* "ash," to blacken her eyebrows. Since the actual clothing worn by a lady was fairly plain, she would have taken special care to decorate herself with jewelry and elaborate hairstyles. A *fibula*, "brooch," was a very common ornament, but Roman women were also adorned with other objects such as *armilla*, "bracelets," and a *focale*, "neck scarf," and maybe even *periscelides*, "ankle bracelets."

insulae
[*in*-sul-ey]
tower blocks

It might be easy to forget, with all the emphasis on the large, multi-chambered *domus*, that there was any other kind of dwelling in the ancient city of Rome, except the grand palaces of the emperor. But the majority of Romans lived somewhere quite different and much closer to the urban living spaces we often see today, that is, in block apartment buildings. *Urbem . . . tenui tibicine fultam*, "a city built on thin flutes," so Juvenal drolly described the precarious structure of the *insulae*.

These apartment blocks were built from wood and mud bricks, so were prone to fire and collapse. Emperor Augustus stepped in and legislated that they could not be higher than 60 feet (18 meters), but these rules were not meticulously followed, and hence Juvenal wrote grimly of the constant wails for water, and of the fires that crept up from ground level, so the last man to burn would have been the poorest, who lived right up amidst the eaves, *molles ubi reddunt ova columbae*, or "where the gentle doves lay their eggs."

In these *insulae*, families were crammed into one room, with no toilet or cooking facilities, and they made regular trips down to the ground level to collect cooked food and clean water, or, if they were less considerate or perhaps more tired, they simply tipped sewage buckets down into the streets below. The soaring rents for these tiny rooms were a frequent source of lamentation in literature and the higher up the tower one went, the more dire and appalling the accommodation.

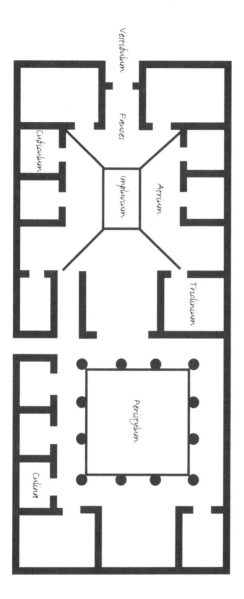

patricii
"elite, native Romans"
augur
"seer"

RES PUBLICA

"public affairs"

From *res publica* we derive our word "republic." It has often been said that the public life of the Romans, which in its loosest definition meant the life spent outside of one's private home, really described what being a Roman was all about. Clearly the most prevalent and profound legacies that the Roman language and culture have left us are our political and legal systems. Their words and ideas have left an enduring impression upon the way many modern societies govern themselves, and on the public life of their cities and towns.

From the looming Capitol and the grand Palatine Hill, to the grubbier, noisier Aventine and the mighty, regal flow of the river Tiber, each of these districts and features said something about the way Roman society was structured and functioned.

The following words and expressions reveal three primary facets of the public life of ancient Rome: politics, religion, and the law. Roman political life is essential to understanding the city and its people, and many entries present information on the roles in public office, and the public buildings.

Intimately bound up with politics in ancient Rome was religion, expressed powerfully by the ubiquitous ruined temples that remain today, and also by the roles of ancient government and religious colleges. For the Romans, superstition and religion were deeply embedded in the workings of public life. While a deeply felt spiritualism seems to have been absent from ancient Rome, religion was nonetheless woven into the fabric of Roman life, and therefore visible and omnipresent in all stratas of society.

Anyone who has had any dealings with our legal system, however small, will recognize the legacy of Latin within it, and not just Latin language. So many of our laws are modeled on or have emerged from the legal system of the Roman Republic and Empire. Rome's developing legal system was something at the very heart of the city and of what it meant to be a citizen. It represented the infancy of human rights. So much of the grandeur and wonder of the civilization of ancient Rome is expressed in these systems.

senatus
[sen-*ah*-tus]
senate

The governing council of the Roman Republic, and the empire it later became, was the Senate. It actually comes from the Latin word for an "old man," *senex*, since the council was meant to be made up of the "elders." According to legend, the first senate in Rome was established by Romulus; it was set up to be an advisory body and initially consisted of the heads of one hundred families.

The Senate did not have executive power; everything had to be voted on in the public assemblies. But with one or two exceptions, its authority meant that its will was carried out. Eventually, the Senate was made up of men selected and appointed by people called *censors*. The Senators were mostly the wealthy and privileged of society, and enjoyed lifelong membership, with a few caveats; if one was found guilty of

Winged Victory collecting votes in an urn, holding an olive branch. Late 3rd century CE Roman mosaic.

offences such as corruption, severe domestic violence, bad treatment of slaves or clients, and certain other egregious acts, then he could be ejected.

quisque faber suae fortunae
[*kwis*-kweh *fab*-er *soo*-ey for-*too*-ney]
each is the architect of his own fortune

Appius Claudius Caecus said these words in the first ever recorded political speech in Latin. He was a Roman politician who introduced various measures to support the lower classes. He also built the Appian Way, which became one of Rome's most important roads and connected Rome to Brindisi, Apulia in the southeast.

senatus populusque Romanus
[sen-*ah*-tus po-pul-*us*-kwe ro-*mah*-nus]
the senate and the people of Rome

When the Romans went into battle, which they did fairly often, they would have the letters SPQR engraved on their shield. This stood for *Senatus Populusque Romanus*, the official name of the Roman Republic, and the motto of the city of Rome today.

curia
[*ku*-ri-a]
The Senate house

The Senate met at a building in the Forum called the *curia*. The word developed from the idea that the Senate offered its *curam*, "care" over the city, and it gives us our words "curious," "cure," and "care" itself.

The *Curia Hostilia* was the original meeting place, an imposing building at the foot of the Capitoline Hill, purposefully built to dominate the Forum and display the strength of the Republic. It was rebuilt once after an angry mob burned it down, and it then remained standing until Julius Caesar tore the building down, and started to build a new one, which was called, rather unsurprisingly, *Curia Julia*. This building was not prominently placed at the center of the Forum, but was more tucked away to one side, a positioning which perhaps unintentionally reflected the demise of the power of the Senate and the erosion of the Republic that was beginning at around that time.

After Julius Caesar was murdered and Augustus, his adopted son, took power, the building was finally finished, and Augustus proudly declared that "I built the Senate House . . . with the power of the state entirely in my hands by universal consent, I extinguished the flames of civil wars, and then relinquished my control," which may have sounded good, but was untrue.

Horse held by its bridle, 3rd century CE Roman mosaic.

equites
[*e*-qui-tays]
knights

The middle classes of ancient Rome were known as *equites*, the root of which is the Latin word *equus*, "horse," since being able to afford one's own horse required a certain amount of wealth. Even once the term had become symbolic rather than literal, it was still very much in currency as a label to position one in society. To be of *equestrian* rank in Augustus' time, one needed the significant sum of 400,000 sesterces. An *eques* also became known as an *egregius vir*, or "outstanding man" in a complex system of labels devised in 2 CE. They were distinguished in dress by a gold ring, and a narrow black band on their tunics.

patricii
[pa-*tri*-ki-ee]
the elite, native Romans

The patricians, from *patres* meaning "fathers," were the upper classes, a group of elite families who made up the Senate. They were privileged in all kinds of ways, including over-representation in public assemblies, and they were even believed to have had some kind of direct communication line to the gods, so originally only patricians could hold religious office. As time went by, during the years of the Republic, greater freedoms and opportunities were granted to members of the lower classes, and some of them rose to greater power and wealth. At the same time some of the old patricians went broke and fell down society's ladders.

plebeii
[ple-*bay*-ee]
common people

The patricians, the native inhabitants of Rome, felt they were superior to new arrivals, who became known as *plebeii* or plebeians. Intermarriage was forbidden, although the plebeians could make their way up the social ladder through gaining wealth and by performing good works for the State. Their lower social status also precluded them from certain official positions. As time went by a *concilium*, "council," was established for plebeians, and thus they were given some limited say over their own lives, but a few hundred years passed before they attained true equality with the Patricians (around 287 BCE). The origin of the word *plebius* is not known, but the term remains in use today, in a less official way, and has become the derisory term "pleb," inferring one has a lack of culture and breeding.

censor
[*ken*-sor]
magistrate

Familiar to English speakers from our word "censored," the title *censor* actually comes from the verb *censeo,* meaning "I value" or "I estimate."

To become a Roman citizen one needed to register on the census; failure to do so could lead to forfeiting possessions and property or even banishment. The state appointed two *censors*, from the aristocracy and men of "impeccable" character, who could be relied upon to make the necessary judgments upon the characters of Roman citizens.

The hierarchy in Rome was based upon material wealth, but a person's behavior in all kinds of spheres was also taken into account: family relationships, actions in society, and personality. It was obviously of great importance where one was placed in the rankings, and some social mixes within the hierarchy were forbidden, but Roman comedy and love elegies suggest these rules were often broken.

vestis virum reddit
[*wes*-tis *wir*-um *red*-dit]
the clothes make the man

A quote by the Roman writer Quintilian, this is still very much
in currency today, and was just as relevant in ancient Rome
as it is now, if not more so. The Romans were acutely aware
of clothing, for it reflected one's status in society. The toga

The Roman poet Virgil, 70–19 BCE, writing the *Aeneid*. The toga he
wears was a mark of a Roman citizen.

was important as it was the mark of a Roman citizen. It was meticulously draped and abundantly folded, so that it fell in just the right way as its owner walked; it was also frequently washed so that it retained its brilliant whiteness, and this meant that it wore out quite quickly and had to be replaced regularly.

Various stripes or borders on the rim of the toga indicated whether one was a Senator or held a role in office, and so on. The Roman poet Virgil put these words into the mouth of the ruler of the gods, Jupiter: "masters of the earth, the race that wears the toga."

aquam dare
[*a*-qwam *dah*-reh]
to give water

A phrase often used by Roman writers in connection to law courts, it refers to the water clock the Romans would sometimes use to tell the time. Sundials were another common method, but they proved less useful indoors, so water clocks were used to measure out how long an advocate could speak, as water would drain from one vessel into another. For serious cases, where execution might have been an option, the water might have been filled to the top to allow more time for discussion; for the less important ones, it might have been only half-filled. This process was "giving water," and therefore time, for the speaker.

forum
[*for*-um]
market place

This word is familiar to us all—constantly reinvented to keep up with time and technology; for example, we have virtual forums on the Internet where enthusiasts will discuss anything from new bike wheels to football teams to the finer points of Western philosophy. And even before our Internet age, we used the term for any venue of debate and discussion. The Forum was one of the most important locations in the ancient city of Rome.

All that remains of it now are ruins of lonely, decayed pillars soaring into the skies, the gaps glaring like missing teeth among the debris of temples once elaborate and perfect; but one can still sense the majesty of the place as it once would have been. The Forum was the beating heart of the Roman city, and therefore of public life. There one found the centers of politics and justice—politicians would give their speeches at *rostra* (platforms), people would come to buy, to sell, to worship, to witness and judge in trials, or even just to chat.

templum Concordiae
[*tem*-plum Kon-*kord*-i-aye]
temple of harmony

Concordia means "harmony," and comes from the Latin prefix *con*, "together," and *cor*, "heart." Early in Roman times, much antagonism existed between the patricians and the plebeians. In the run up to the Punic Wars (264 BCE) some laws were finally floated for equal rights for both classes.

The patricians were not at all pleased about this, but the laws were finally accepted, and the consul at the time had a temple built and dedicated to the goddess of harmony, Concordia. This was placed prominently in the Forum to remind people of the reconciliation as they went about their daily lives.

duodecim tabulae
[*dou*-o-dek-im *tab*-you-ley]
twelve tables

The Twelve Tables were the basis of Roman law, and were displayed in the Forum for all to see. There was a time when the pontiffs kept these laws highly secret, punishing plebeians horrifically for offences they hadn't known they'd committed, with punishments they hadn't imagined could exist. This sort of behavior couldn't last, and eventually after a long campaign, the Patricians agreed to the laws being written down and displayed for all to see.

Unfortunately, we don't have much left of them, only quotes and some extracts from various authors. Strangely, what we do have seems to have been written in a childish, sing-song style, perhaps to allow the common people, who were largely illiterate, to better understand and remember the weighty laws.

While some of the laws seem perfectly reasonable—for example, if someone died, or went mad, their property went to the next of kin—others seem bizarre and brutal by today's standards. For example, we have a fragment of one law referring to actions of people who cast spells on other people's land, and another which states that children born with deformities should be put to death.

atrium vestae
[*a*-tri-um *wes*-tey]
hall of Vesta

One of the most fascinating traditions in ancient Rome was the Vestal Virgins. Their existence has captured people's imaginations ever since, to the extent that we still use the expression "vestal" to refer to the continuation of an ancient tradition.

The Vestal Virgins were a team of women in charge of keeping the fire burning in the temple of Vesta, goddess of the Hearth. This temple was located in the Forum, as was the

A Roman mosaic in the city of Carthage representing a Roman vestal.

home of its attendants, the *atrium vestae*. These women were selected as little girls for 30 years of service: 10 years as students, 10 in service, and then finally 10 as teachers. Throughout this time, they were considered to be daughters of Rome, and were sworn to a vow of chastity (hence the name) that had fatal consequences if it was broken.

If one of the Vestal Virgins had sexual relations with anyone, she was buried alive in an underground chamber with only a few days worth of food and water. The method for determining whether the woman in question had transgressed her vows was to check whether the sacred fire had gone out. But this did not deter parents from wanting their daughters to be selected, because the advantages of being a Vestal Virgin were considerable. Since they weren't subject to a man, in the form of either father or husband, they had a degree of independence that other women in Roman society did not; for example, they could own property and also vote. They also had considerable political influence—the emperor would consult them on all important matters, and they could even get people pardoned. Their well-being was seen to be inextricably tied to the good of the city, and hence they were protected and cared for.

After their 30 years service had ended, they had the option to leave and get married, but many of them enjoyed the wealth, comfort, power, and freedom that came with their position as a Vestal Virgin, and chose to continue this lifestyle rather than surrender their freedom for a life with a man.

pontifex maximus
[*pon*-ti-feks *mak*-sim-us]
chief priest

The word *pontifex* literally means a "bridge builder," and this particular term, "the greatest bridge builder," was the name of the high priest of the most important religious order of the Roman state, the *collegium pontificum*, "College of Pontiffs." Although of course the chief priest did not go around building bridges, there is a theory that this term did once have a more literal meaning, since the river Tiber flowing through Rome was treated as a deity, and only religious authorities could attempt to construct anything in or over it.

Bridge building in its metaphorical sense was also no doubt intended, as the priests were seen as building a sort of bridge between the divine and mortal worlds, communicating with the gods, offering them sacrifices, and praying to them. Politics and religion were deeply connected, and by the time of the Roman Empire, the emperor himself took up the post of high priest. The term is still sometimes used to refer to Popes.

augur
[*aw*-ger]
seer

We've all heard people call something "auspicious," referring to some sign or impression that an event is not going according to plan. The term actually derives from the job of certain individuals in the ancient world known as *augurs*, thought to come from the verb *augeo*, "I increase," which gives us our word "augment." These men were part of the official college of priests in Rome, and their job was to look at birds. They examined their flights, squawks, comings, and goings, and then would make notes and draw conclusions about various decisions that had been taken by the people of power in the city. This process was called "taking auspices." Leaders would consult *augurs* before doing just about anything.

haruspex
[*har*-u-speks]
neomancer

Sometimes you have to get your hands dirty to do things properly and the *haruspex* was one man who knew the literal truth of this. The *haruspex* had to cut open a sheep or other sacrificial animal, fish around for the entrails, and then examine them for signs about the future. They particularly looked at the size, shape, and color of the animal's liver, and through these signs they interpreted the will of the gods on important decisions such as whether to go to war.

The practice stretched back far before the Romans, since the Babylonians and Etruscan civilizations practiced the art. The notion seems to derive from an ancient belief that the liver produced blood, and was therefore the font of life.

Mons Palatinus
[*Mons* Pa-la-*ti*-nus]
Palatine Hill

The Palatine Hill was the most exclusive of the seven hills on which Rome was built, and from it we derive our word "palace" and "palatial." It loomed over the Forum, and the views and clear air it provided were of great appeal to those with money, so it became the place where the wealthy citizens lived. The writer Ovid based his vision of the home of the most important of the gods on the Palatine: "on evenings when deepest heavens are clear, one sees a high road called The Milky Way where gods walk out upon a path of stars to Jove the thunderer; on either side of palace and high hall, great doors fall open to the chambered light; guests wandering where Nobility receives its worshippers. The lesser deities do not live here." And if it wasn't obvious enough, he even cheekily added "I choose to call it Palatine of Heaven."

Emperors built their lavish homes there, each one competing to construct something more ostentatiously elaborate than the last. Augustus was born there, and legend also has it that this was where Romulus and Remus were raised by a she-wolf before being adopted by shepherds. The oldest area of Rome, excavations indicate that people had settled there as long ago as 1000 BCE.

si deus si dea
[si *de*-us si *de*-uh]
whether a god or a goddess

A famous tomb has been found on the Palatine Hill with an inscription starting with these words. The practice of starting dedications by including all possibilities for the deity was a common one—we find prayers with lengthy lists of all the many names one might have used for a particular god; people felt the divinity might be angered if one happened to misname him (or her), get his (or her) gender wrong, or make any other similar mistakes. To avoid this, the Romans decided to just include everything they could. For this particular tomb, we don't have enough evidence to determine to whom it was dedicated, so it has remained a mystery to this day. It is simply known as "altar for an unknown deity."

Bona Dea
[*bon*-uh *de*-uh]
good goddess

On the Aventine Hill—the rough and ready district of the city, where gangs warred and poorer people got on with their daily grind—one would find the temple and garden of the so-called "good goddess." She was a very popular deity with slaves and the lower classes, and was often approached with requests for healing, but her primary and most important public role was her perceived power for women and fertility.

A woman in ancient Rome was viewed and valued for her ability to have children, and so being infertile was bad news. This virgin goddess was the one to pray to if a woman was having problems of that nature. She was said to be the daughter of Faunus, who apparently once beat her with a stick of myrtle after she came home drunk—for this reason, the words "myrtle" and "wine" were banned at her rites, in case she was still feeling a bit sensitive about the matter. Snakes were her special symbol, representing her roles in both healing and fertility. There were specially consecrated snakes kept at her temple, where people would visit to be healed and helped.

Every year on December 4, her secret rites would be performed at the house of the *pontifex maximus* or another senior magistrate. Men were barred from the proceedings, and even pictures of men, or male animals, or anything remotely masculine were outlawed. No one really knows what happened at these rites as they were deeply secret, but when a man named Publius Clodius was alleged to have gatecrashed, it caused quite a commotion in Roman public life.

Naked woman surrounded by roses, 2nd century CE mosaic.

compitalia
[com-pit-*ah*-li-uh]
festival of the crossroad gods

So much of city life in ancient Rome, as in our cities today, was segregated into districts that had their own flavors and rituals, ways and wiles. But just as we have our big street carnivals which unite people, the *compitalia*—from the word *compitum* meaning "crossroad"—was the festival that brought the Romans together. It was put on for the gods of crossroads and took place at any point where two roads met, so all sorts of people would come together to worship at this event. These gods were an aspect of the *Lares*, the household gods, and were worshipped for protection.

The festival took place in January (though the exact date varied). People were said to have brought honey-cakes and woolen dolls representing people to give to the Lares of the crossroads. At some point Tarquinius Superbus, the last of the kings of Rome, interpreted the words of an oracle to mean that people should sacrifice the heads of children instead of these woolen dolls. This gruesome practice did not last for long though, as Brutus, who overthrew the Tarquins in a classic political maneuver, determined that the oracle had only specified "heads," so the festival goers were allowed to pick something rather less animate, and chose poppy and garlic heads instead.

quid agis?

[kwid *ag*-is]

how are you?

Meaning literally "what are you leading/driving," this was the Latin equivalent in ancient Rome for "how are you doing?" or the more informal "what's up?" There are many instances in literature of the time showing us that people regularly greeted each other in this way.

ad Kalendas Graecas

[ad kal-*end*-as *Gray*-kas]

to the Greek Kalends

The *Kalendae* were the first days of the Roman months, meaning literally "those called," and giving us our word "calendar," among others. They were measured from the start of a new moon cycle, and on the Kalends people who owed money had to pay it back, since debts were written down in a book known as a *calendria*. The Romans had a complicated system of measurements of dates based in relation to the Kalends, Nones, and Ides, the key days in every month. These were fixed dates, but they had originally been based on lunar conditions.

The Greeks did not use the Kalends, and perhaps the Romans felt it unlikely that their more philosophically minded neighbors would ever be interested in such a perplexing and meticulous system; so they coined the phrase *ad Kalendas Graecas*, meaning something like "until the Greeks use Kalends," to refer to something that was never likely to happen, much like our phrase "till hell freezes over."

ad unguem factus homo
[ad *un*-gwem *fak*-tus *hom*-oh]
a man polished to the nail

Horace, the Roman poet and satirist, coined this expression to describe an individual who paid meticulous attention to his appearance. In today's terms, a business man wearing the best suits and most expensive cufflinks, with not a hair out of place, would be worthy of the description. In the image-conscious world of Rome, appearance was of even greater importance than it is in much of society today. The expression itself derives from the fact that artists who worked with clay and other such materials, molding statues and busts, would take the greatest care over their labors, and finish off the delicate details with their fingernails.

aegrescit medendo
[ay-*gres*-kit med-*en*-doh]
the disease worsens with treatment

So the Roman poet Virgil stated in book twelve of his epic, the *Aeneid*, and it seems that in the case of ancient medicine, this was a common consequence. Some of the ideas and remedies used, while sounding baffling, turned out to be based on sound principles, for example, using cobwebs as plasters for wounds (it turns out they possess healing constituents after all). But there were many others that were much more dubious, such as bleeding people who had fevers.

Pliny wrote of the immense popularity (and fees) of physicians from Greece who swanned around the town attracting crowds of admiring people, and expressed his suspicion of the latest new-fangled medicines and treatments: "I pass over many famous physicians men like Cassius, Calpetanus, Arruntius, and Rubrius. 250,000 sesterces were their annual incomes from the emperors. There is no doubt that all these physicians in their hunt for popularity by means of some new idea, did not hesitate to buy it with our lives. Medicine changes everyday, and we are swept along on the puffs of clever brains of the Greeks . . . as if thousands of people do not live without physicians— though not, of course, without medicine." Nonetheless Pliny himself suggested the cure of tying "warm sheep's lung" around a person's temples to treat a frenzied mental state.

tabula rasa
[*tab*-you-luh *ra*-suh]
scraped tablet

We define this expression today as "a clean slate," but it derives from the Roman method of writing on wax tablets using a stick to carve the letters, and then scraping it clear again. These tablets were commonly used in schools attended by the children of wealthy families.

panem et circenses
"bread and circuses"
pollice verso
"turned thumb"

ARS LONGA, VITA BREVIS

"art is long, life is short"

This has been attributed to the poet Horace as a Latin version of a phrase from the Greek physician Hippocrates. It's often been said that we can admire the Romans for the splendor of their civilization, with its mighty conquering prowess, and the practicality of their cities, the orderly and refined stateliness of their buildings, temples, and roads; but for all that is artistic and beautiful we look to the Greeks, as in fact the Romans themselves did.

Undeniably the Romans were vastly influenced by the Greek civilization, with all its mystery and sublimity, its almost otherworldly qualities. However, to dismiss Roman culture as derivative and lacking in inspiration and flair would be a mistake. Latin literature, for example, has produced a poetic elegance and vision.

The greatest paradox about the culture of ancient Rome that emerges is the juxtaposition of the gruesome barbarity of some aspects of Roman civilization—such as the gladiatorial games, the public executions, the animal and slave fights—with the subtlety and refined pleasures of so much of their art, literature, theater, music, and architecture. The worst and the best of humanity seemed to have existed side by side in Rome without causing any sense of cultural unease—the sordid depths of cruelty and depravity next to the exquisite heights of beauty and humanity.

The Romans had a clear sense of the fact that human life could easily be destroyed; indeed they frequently seemed to celebrate and revel in this very fact, but alongside that, they were acutely aware of the more permanent role art of all kinds had in society and history. This chapter provides an insight to what made the Romans tick, what was close to their heart, and what they thought was good entertainment.

panem et circenses
[*pa*-nem et ker-*ken*-says]
bread and circuses

This famous phrase, coined scathingly by Juvenal, has stayed with us throughout the centuries. Today we commonly use it to describe a government's cynical attempts to distract or dupe its citizens by populist policies of various kinds.

Juvenal was lamenting the fact that he felt the people had given up their freedoms and become dependent and interested only in cheap entertainment and the free grain dole, *annona*, which emperors had long exploited as a method of gaining popularity among the people of Rome.

circus maximus
[*ker*-kus *mak*-si-mus]
the largest circus

In ancient Rome, the name *circus* referred to the round shape of
the building where chariot races, horse races, and battles were
the main exhibits. Our words "circuit" and "circle" derive from
this term. Nowadays our circuses contain entertainers such
as trapeze artists and acrobats, an evolution of the older, less
humane versions involving freak shows and animal tricks.

The first venue of this kind in the city of ancient Rome was
located between the Palatine Hill, where the stars of the Roman
world lived, and the Aventine Hill, which was a much poorer
area. Apparently the thing that could unite rich and poor was
violent entertainment. The venue was used by the first kings
of Rome, and then expanded by Julius Caesar in 50 BCE so
that some 250,000 spectators could be seated within it, and
that number again could line the hills, watch, cheer, and jeer
from afar. After that, successive emperors vied to outdo their
predecessors by expanding it further; the emperor Domitian
even decided to build his palace so that it adjoined the Circus,
and he could watch the events from the comfort of his home.
The emperor Trajan made the emperor's seating area larger,
too, so that he could be seen watching the games. Emperors
such as Julius Caesar, who reluctantly attended, damaged their
popularity with such indifference to the games.

The main event was chariot racing, which was a fast, exciting,
and brutal sport. Competitors frequently suffered serious

injuries or died, providing a thrill factor for the spectators. It's not all that different from motor sports today, where excitement over the magnificence of the vehicles and the lunatic speeds is bound up with the possibility of disaster at any moment.

quadrigae
[*quad*-ri-gey]
four-horse chariots

Races involving four-horse chariots were the most popular and therefore important at Roman games. The word is formed from *quadri,* "four," and *iugeo,* "I join," and the chariots often represented victory and divinity. The god Apollo, who had jurisdiction over the sun, was said to have such a chariot, and there are various sculptures of them to be seen in several countries today.

There was a central track, a *spina*, and gates, or *carceres*, from where the chariots would start their race at one end of the circus. When the emperor dropped a bit of cloth known as a *mappa*, the gates would open and the races would begin. This created a fair start for all the competitors. The race got rather less fair after that, when charioteers would take great pains to upset the course of others, but this all added to the excitement and risk involved. The two turns at either end of the track were *metae*, and this was where the worst crashes usually occurred.

The races were free for the poor, and they were extremely popular. The race itself was seven laps, and spectators would bet on the outcome. The racers wore protective helmets, but also took the dangerous measure of tying the reins around their waists, which led to some horrific injuries and fatalities, when a driver got dragged around the course. The drivers would carry a knife to cut themselves free in these instances. All one needed to do to become a celebrity in this field was simply to survive for a while—the dangerous, violent nature of the sport meant that drivers, and their horses, tended to die quickly. From the words *navis*, "ship," and *frango*, "I break," *naufragium* was the term used for a particularly startling and catastrophic chariot crash in the races that left the charioteer and his horse incapacitated, and the chariot destroyed.

The four-horse quadriga race in Circus Maximus, late 3rd–early 4th century CE, Piazza Armerina, Sicily, Italy.

nec te nobilium fugiat certamen equorum

[nek tay no-*bil*-i-um *fou*-gee-at *kert*-a-men eq-*wor*-um]

don't forget the races

In his handbook on romance, the Roman poet Ovid informed his readers that the races were an ideal place for picking up girls, describing the way in which the spectators were packed tightly together in the Circus: "Don't forget the races, those noble stallions: the Circus holds room for a vast obliging crowd. No need here for fingers to give secret messages, nor a nod of the head to tell you she accepts: You can sit by your lady: nothing's forbidden, press your thigh to hers, as you can do, all the time: and it's good the rows force you close, even if you don't like it, since the girl is touched through the rules of the place."

Of course Ovid was eventually exiled for precisely this sort of cheeky advice, but he draws attention to an important and noteworthy fact, which was that the races were the only place where men and women were not segregated. They could sit and watch side by side. His poem also suggests the popularity of the event for both women and men alike, which is another indicator of how central the sport was to Roman life.

Colosseum

[Kol-os-*see*-um]

Colosseum

The Colosseum is one of the defining features of Rome today, and one of the most striking and powerful reminders and symbols of all that we have come to believe about the Romans. It is generally thought that the name comes from a statue of the emperor Nero that had been built beside it—the Romans called any statue that was larger than life-size *colossus*—but its original name was the *Amphitheatrum Flavium*, since the structure was built by the emperors Vespasian and Titus, members of the Flavian dynasty, and was completed by 80 CE. Standing in its ruins today, the magnificent skeleton of the original building is a haunting monument to one of the most

Gladiators fighting, one armed with a whip, the other with a baton, from scenes of gladiatorial combat in the Augusta Treverorum arena, a large main room mosaic, from 2nd–3rd century CE.

famous and horrific aspects of the ancient Roman way of life: the gladiatorial games.

The original floor of the *arena* has worn away, so the cells of animals and slaves underground can be viewed from above, just as the added dimension of time has allowed us to observe the building and its events from a broader and deeper perspective.

The building was constructed at the heart of Rome, representing its centrality to Roman culture, and it seated about 50,000 people. It was elliptical in design, and sand was spread over the fighting ground to soak up the blood. The spectators were given numbered pottery shards upon entering according to where they would be seated. Just as in the hierarchy of Roman society, the seating order was rigidly stratified. Senators would get the best seats at the front, with the *equites* above them, then the wealthier citizens, who were followed higher up by the poor. There was a special box at the top for slaves, women, and the very poor. There were even a few sectors of society that were entirely banned from the Colosseum due to their low standing in society, such as gravediggers, former gladiators, and actors.

naumachiae
[now-*mak*-i-ey]
sea battles

Naumachiae comes straight into Latin from the Greek. Writers of the time recorded that the Colosseum was occasionally used to stage reenactments of famous sea battles. No one is entirely sure of the accuracy of these claims, since such a feat as flooding the Colosseum would have offered all kinds of practical difficulties—especially considering the fact that the building was probably not watertight.

pollice verso
[*pol*-li-keh *wer*-so]
turned thumb

The main events held at the Colosseum were shows, *munera*, put on by private citizens, consisting of gladiators fighting. These shows evolved from funeral rites, in which a *munus*, or "duty," was paid to a dead ancestor to keep his memory alive; when the rulers realized that having prisoners fight to the death was much more entertaining than merely killing them outright on the tombs of dead leaders, they developed the beginning of the most popular entertainment in ancient Roman. Gladiators were often prisoners and slaves, but some were also sons of Roman citizens who had elected themselves for the role, either for the money or the prestige.

Once chosen, gladiators would be trained in a school attached to the Colosseum, and prepared for a life of fighting. As it happens, gladiators rarely fought to the death: one or the other would surrender or be clearly defeated. The emperor (encouraged by the crowd) could then choose to spare or end the life of the loser, with the famous *pollice verso*, meaning "turned thumb" (no one's really sure which way it was turned).

Prior to the fights, programs were distributed to the audience containing biographies of the fighters, and information on who was fighting, who had been fighting, and who had died, was often written up on walls or in a daily newspaper. Spectators liked to support a particular gladiator, and on days when famous ones were fighting, ticket scalpers would sell seats at an extortionate rate. The fights usually happened in early evening, preceded by various executions, animal fights or hunts, and other such entertainments. The upper classes would usually leave before the executions, since to watch one was considered distasteful. They were, however, more than happy to watch slaves ripping each other to shreds.

When a gladiator was killed, as sometimes happened by accident, two men dressed up as Charon, the mythical character who exported dead souls to the underworld, and Mercury, the divine messenger of the gods, would take away the body. They would be sure to slit his throat first, though, to catch out any fakers. Music would also be played, often by musicians dressed up as bears, birds, and other creatures, to add a dramatic soundtrack to the proceedings.

sylvae
[*sil*-wey]
mythological countryside scenes

These were recreations of countryside scenery inside the arena, such as forest and woodland idylls, often brilliantly rendered by painters and architects, to please the crowds and punctuate performances of more brutal, sparse images. Wild animals of various kinds, ranging from hippos and elephants to leopards and ostriches would sometimes be let into the scenes. If that sounds rather charming and innocent, these backdrops were also often used to depict violent death scenes, where the mythological figure would be played by an unfortunate prisoner who would then be mauled to death or killed in some equally horrible way.

ludi romani
[*lou*-dee ro-*mah*-nee]
games

The *ludi Romani* was a Roman religious festival in honor of Jupiter, which took place every year at some point in September

Mosaic of a tragic theater mask with festoons of fruit and flowers. ca. 100 CE from a Roman villa at Rabat, Malta.

(although the exact date isn't known). *Ludi* gives us words such as "illusion," "prelude," and "delude."

Intially, the games appear to have been a one-day event, but the date they were held seems to have been affected by political currents and events, such as the expulsion or assassination of an emperor, and it shifted or extended accordingly. The festival would have started off with a *pompa*, a "procession," and then there would have been chariot races and contests. But it wasn't just sporting events; Greek drama was also introduced to Rome at this festival. The plays were funded by the state, and were free to everyone. A particular magistrate could supplement the fee paid by the state to create a more successful play, and there were suggestions that this often meant magistrates would pay members of the audience to clap wildly, to give the impression that the play was better than it might actually have been. There were also other events going on, from acrobats to animal-baiting, which grew increasingly popular as literary drama waned.

Games were also part of other public yearly festivals celebrated in the name of a particular god or goddess. Examples include festivals such as the *ludi Megalenses*, an April vegetation-based event in honor of the "Great Mother," and the *ludi Florales*, in honor of Flores, the goddess of Spring plants and crops.

theatrum
[te-*ah*-trum]
seeing place

Our word "theater" comes from the Latin word *theatrum*, which in turn came from the ancient Greek word *theatrum*, meaning a "seeing place," and in fact, much of ancient Roman theater was directly derived from the great Greek plays, their texts, their methods of performing them, and even the layout of the theaters.

The buildings themselves were semi-circular in form, and consisted of a stage, orchestra, and audience area, *auditorium*, from the verb *audio*, "I listen." Entrances known as *vomitoria* at the edges of the seating area allowed the audience to get in and out. The *auditorium* was usually set into a hill or slope, allowing a staggered seating layout, and a *scaenae frons*—a wall at the back of the stage for scenery—provided an air of realism.

Roman plays were by and large comedies rather than the profound and haunting tragedies that the ancient Greeks were famous for. A trip to the theater was frequently raucous and boisterous—the audience would actively participate, booing and cheering and calling out insulting comments. The noise was so disruptive that the plays themselves accommodated this by including a lot of repetition, and allowed for the fact that the words of the actors often could not be heard by incorporating mime into the acting style.

fabula palliata
[*fab*-oo-luh pal-li-*ah*-tuh]
play in Greek dress

This expression defines Roman drama, which was usually performed in Greek dress and according to Greek customs. It comes from *pallium*, the Latin word for a Greek cloak, and *fabula*, a story or play (which also gives us our words "fable" and "fabulous"). The works of playwrights Plautus and Terence were both performed in this way.

Theatrical masks. A Roman mosaic from Villa Adriana in Rome, Italy.

The Romans were more interested in the visual effects of the theater, rather than the religious significance that the Greeks strove to invoke in their plays. One of the innovations the Romans introduced was a color code for the robes to indicate who the characters were meant to be. For example, an actor wearing yellow was playing the part of a woman, someone wearing white was an old man, and purple robes signified a young man.

There were also important symbols included in their appearance that told the audience more about the character, such as a yellow tassel that marked out the actor as a god. Given that one of the Romans' favorite humorous techniques in their comedies was a case of a god being mistaken for a mortal, this would have been hidden or removed for most of the play. There was also something called *comœdia togata*, "toga-ed comedy," which was performed, as the name suggests, in Roman dress.

acta est fabula plaudite

[*ak*-tuh est *fab*-oo-luh plow-*di*-tay]
the play has finished: applaud

These words are often to be found at the end of Roman comedies, which may or may not give us some indication of what Augustus thought of his life, since he was meant to have said these as his last words. The idea was to alert the audience that this was the end, rather than having an awkward moment of uncertainty as to whether to burst into applause or not.

flamma fumo est proxima
[*flam*-muh *fou*-mo est *proks*-i-muh]
flame is close to smoke

This is one of many famous quotes from the Roman comedic playwright Plautus, from his play *Curculio*, familiar in our own version of the saying, "no smoke without fire." In the play these words are spoken as a warning to another character that one thing follows on from another—in this case, while kissing a girl might seem perfectly innocent and chaste, it will lead on to worse things and people will get burned.

Many of Plautus' comedies were actually lifted from the ancient Greek playwright Menander, and they often focused on recurring themes and plots such as the relationship between father and son, mistaken identities, and young men falling in love with the wrong girl and all of the problems and consequences that then arose.

floralia
[flo-*rah*-li-uh]
flower

The *Floralia* was a festival in honor of the goddess Flora. Much as our holidays are governed by festivals of religious observances, such as Christmas and Easter, so the ancient Romans had a series of festivals that punctuated working life, and that consisted of various community and family events. However, for the Romans these were far more about public entertainment and community involvement than our main festivals have become.

Floralia was celebrated at the end of April through the first few days of May, and as Flora was a goddess of spring vegetation, offerings of flowers were made to her. People would abandon their more customary white clothes, and wear a variety of colors. The festival itself consisted of a lot of merriment, wild games, theater, and mime.

The festival was canceled for a time, but a few successive years of bad weather followed, which damaged the blossoms. This was attributed to the wrath of the goddess for canceling her festival, and it was reinstated.

Io Saturnalia!
[*Yo* Sat-er-*nay*-li-uh]
Ho Saturnalia!

This was the most popular of the Roman festivals, so-called from the fact that it celebrated the dedication of the temple of Saturn. It gives us our adjective "Saturnalian," which describes any event that is decadent and merry. *Io Saturnalia* was the greeting that Romans would exchange with one another, and it has also been found graffitied onto walls. It was a winter festival, and many aspects are thought to have been the basis for some of our Christmas traditions, such as the giving and receiving of presents.

Probably the most striking aspect, though, was the reversal of roles. During Saturnalia, the slave and master would, to some extent, switch places. The slave would treat the master with disrespect, and would not be punished for anything, and everyone would wear the hat of a freed man. Colorful dinner clothes were worn instead of plain white togas.

tantaene animis caelestibus irae?
[*tan*-tey-neh *an*-im-ees key-*les*-ti-bus *ir*-ey]
did such anger come from the hearts of gods?

Virgil wrote the most famous piece of Roman literature, the epic poem *Aeneid*. The scourge of school children even in his own time, it tells the story of the founding of Rome, from the ashes of Troy to the beginnings of the mighty empire, culminating in the so-called Augustan golden age, during which time Virgil was alive. It included a trip to the underworld, fierce battles, a love affair, some troublesome gods, and fantastic phrases.

A contradiction seems to lie at the heart of this ostensibly patriotic work, though, which conveys the poet's dilemma; it appears to champion the civilized character of the Roman people and yet ends with a display of wanton violence and revenge on behalf of its hero, Aeneas. The quote above is in the opening lines of the poem and expresses Virgil's own tormented feelings at his poem's vision of the world.

cithara
[kith-*ah*-ruh]
a type of lyre

The *cithara* was a musical instrument, like a seven-stringed lyre, used in ancient Rome by professional singers. From it descends both the idea and the name of our modern instrument, the "guitar." Other popular instruments in Rome were a lute (a three-stringed version of the *cithara* which was easier to play), tuba (a long trumpet) and the *aulos* (flute).

The Romans even had *ascaules*, which were the ancient equivalent of bagpipes. Little is known about ancient Roman music—the assumptions we have about what it might have sounded like and how they might have played it, are based on the supposition that since the Romans took most of their creative ideas from the Greeks, they probably imported Greek music similarly. However it does seem that music was an important aspect of public festivals and plays, as well as a big part of private entertainment in the home.

Musician playing panpipes, from the Museo della Civilta Romana, Rome, 2nd century CE.

sesquipedalia verba
[ses-*kwi*-ped-*ah*-li-uh *wer*-buh]
words a foot-and-a-half long

Verba, "words," of course gives us our words "verb" and "verbose," but *sesquipedalia* is rather an amalgamation of different words. The Roman poet Horace, clearly having had enough of awful attempts at verse from would-be poets, decided it would be a good idea to pen a piece on how exactly to write a good poem. One of the many tendencies he commented upon is the one alluded to in this ironic phrase—verbose, obscure, lengthy words that didn't add anything to the poem.

nunc Roma est aurea
[nunk *Rom*-uh est *ow*-re-uh]
now Rome is golden

Ovid, born a little later than Virgil, had a much more playful edge to his poetry, and among his poems one can find a selection of tongue-in-cheek love poems, a guide for lovers and would-be lovers, and his startling and multilayered epic, the *Metamorphoses*, which incorporates change at every level of its narrative, to brilliant and often hilarious effect. The *enfant terrible* of the Roman poetical world, he eventually got himself banished to the farthest reaches of the Roman Empire and spent the rest of his life writing long, pleading reams on his sorrows.

The quote above, from his work *Ars Amatoria*, displays his witty and gently subversive take on the world he lived in,

suggesting as it does that the golden age of Augustus was s[o]
called because of all the wealth the Romans had amassed for
themselves through their campaigns and conquests. In a time
when poets cultivated an elite attitude toward their audiences,
Ovid shamelessly catered to the popular taste of ordinary
citizens—perhaps the reason why Augustus chose to make an
example of him.

gutta cavat lapidem non vi sed saepe cadendo
[*goot*-tuh *cah*-wat *la*-pid-em nohn wi sed *sey*-peh ca-*den*-doh]
a drop hollows a stone not by force, but by falling often

The Roman poet Ovid wrote these words in one of the poems
he composed after having been exiled by Augustus, many of
which consisted of pleas of various kinds to be allowed home.
This drip-drip technique didn't seem to work with the emperor,
though, since Ovid eventually died in exile.

difficile est saturam non scribere
[dif-*fik*-il-eh est sat-*ur*-am nohn *skri*-be-reh]
it is difficult not to write satire

So said Juvenal, whose sharp, biting take on the life and times of
ancient Rome won him fame if not money. He had something
biting to say on almost every topic. Horace and Juvenal were the
most famous of the Roman satirists; Juvenal's acerbic and bitter
take on Roman society contrasted with Horace's more mellow

e perspective. The term "satire" itself, seems
from *satura lanx,* which literally meant "a full
mean "a mixed dish of fruits" and referred to
ted nature of the original satire writing.

Erato, the Muse of lyric poetry. 2nd–3rd century CE mosaic, from a
villa at Augusta Trevorum (Treves).

lapides in Eumolpum recitantem miserunt

[lap-*id*-ays in Yoo-*mol*-pum re-ki-*tant*-em *mis*-er-unt]

they threw stones at Eumolpus reciting

So Petronius, the Roman writer, described the rather aggressive reaction of a crowd to a poet who has pitched up to recite his verse in public. The public recital was one of the ways for authors to assert themselves. These would sometimes happen in the homes of the wealthy, in private readings with friends, but the more ambitious or desperate would set up in a corner of the forum and attract an audience, and perhaps some stray projectiles, that way.

Recitals such as these were important as there were very few other means to get one's work heard by the public. In a time when mass printing was not even a distant dream, the closest a person could get to having their beloved work published for others to read was to have a team of scribes, employed by a bookseller, copy it all out for them. Even if an aspiring writer had this method available to him, the scope for errors, misreadings, and bored, rebellious slaves inserting rude words into one's script was reasonably large.

tali

[*tal*-i]

knucklebones

This was the Latin name for the "knucklebones," and also referred to a game, more popular in Greece than Rome, that involved throwing the knucklebones of sheep. The values one, three, four, and six were ascribed to the four sides, which, though not usually marked, were recognized instead by their particular shapes relating to the concave and convex shapes of the bones. The various throws seemed to have been named after gods, heroes, and other such famous figures. It was recorded that the emperor Augustus had said that throwing a one, a *canis*, or a six, a *senio*, meant that the player had to put a *denarius* into the pot, and the player who managed to throw a Venus, which was said to be a one, three, four, six, would win the pot and everything in it.

The Romans also played a game called *Tropa*, which involved simply trying to throw knucklebones into a pot without any complex scoring system.

latrunculi
[lah-*truhn*-koo-lee]
robber-soldiers

Just as we might bring out the Monopoly board or Trivial Pursuit, so the Romans had their own versions of board games to entertain them. They would have played these games at feasts and dinners in their homes, such as *tabulae,* similar to backgammon, or a strategic game a little bit like chess, which they called *latrunculi.*

The most popular game was *latrunculi.* It was played, it seems, on a board of variable size, but the ones most commonly found have been twelve squares by eight. Players had 17 pieces with which to play, and could place these, two at a time, anywhere they wanted to on the board and use these pieces to capture pieces belonging to their opponent. There is some debate as to whether the game was played with one type of piece or two—the accounts of the game by ancient writers vary, and perhaps the rules of the game also evolved over time.

mimus
[*mi*-mus]
mime

Giving us our words "mime" and "mimicking," it will come as no surprise that this was a type of farcical drama in ancient Rome, which included a lot of mimickry and absurd characterizations of people. It started off as an alternative to the more formalized and unrealistic theater experience of the traditional plays, with their masks and various conventions. Mime was far more natural, there were no masks, and on occasion, no clothes.

in digito clavus
"nail in my toe"
sterculinium publicum!
"you public toilet!"

VOX POPULI

"the voice of the people"

The origin of this Latin expression is a matter of debate; no one is quite sure of where and when it was first used, but its meaning is well known.

Much of what remains to us of the Romans is a representation of their vast wealth and power, their rulers, their poets and historians, their army, their architects—essentially, the upper echelons of their society. When the Roman poet Ovid wrote his dramatic and confident sign off to his epic poem *Metamorphoses*, "wherever Rome extends its sway, I will live," he was writing with the privilege and confidence of the wealthy elite. For the enormous majority who swarmed the narrow main streets of Rome, writing poetry wasn't an option, for the simple reason that most of the Roman population was illiterate. The gap between rich and poor was vast, and we are often so mesmerized by the splendid ruins of the mighty buildings and the elegant grandeur of the poetry and speeches of the elite that we forget the overwhelming majority of people who have left no such clear marks for us to read and observe. Yet there are fragments and clues that we can use to discover the daily lives of the common people. Writers describing the city of ancient Rome often give away precious details in their sketches; artists paint elements that communicate something of the way people lived, mosaics likewise. Paintings, for example, commonly depicted gods and goddesses, famous battle scenes, and triumphs. But members of the Roman elite would also have paintings in their homes which showed the people on the street, such as depictions of beggars and drunk old women, which provides us with a bit more context and background for life in the city. Graffiti and inscriptions of other kinds are vitally important; just as today they convey messages to us about the people of those streets if we know how to interpret them; they were the voice of those in society who had no other means of expression, and as such, it told us what mattered to the average person in Rome, from which politicians they supported, to how they verbally abused one another and those in authority.

Sources like these have helped us form a clearer, more colorful picture of what life in Rome was really like for the majority.

Helena amatur a Rufo
[*Hel*-en-*uh* am-ah-tur a *Rouf*-oh]
Rufus loves Helena

Graffiti is one of the most important areas of evidence we have for how most people lived in ancient Rome. Access to paper was not easy, since the only equivalent was highly expensive *papyri*, a material made from reeds, so people would express their love, hate, anger, and excitement at the general flow of daily life in inscriptions on walls. Political slogans, addresses of local prostitutes, and quotes from famous poetry appeared alongside sexual bragging, laundry lists, and woeful declarations of broken hearts, or worse still, unwanted pregnancies. One inscription gives the address of a woman named Novellia Primigenia of Nuceria, a prostitute, apparently of great beauty, whose services were much in demand. Another shows a phallus accompanied by the text, *mansueta tene,* "handle with care."

Often these would end with warnings such as, "Don't erase this or may you get really ill!" One ironic inscription on a wall exclaimed, *admiror paries te non cecidisse ruinis qui tot scriptorum taedia sustineas,* "I am amazed, wall, that you haven't collapsed from all these foul inscriptions."

frontem tabernae sopionibus scribam
[*fron*-tem tab-*ur*-ney sop-i-*oh*-ni-bus *skri*-bam]
I will draw *sopios* on the front of the tavern

We learn a lot of the most appalling and profane uses of Latin in ancient Rome from the Roman poet Catullus, who as well as writing beautiful, moving, and heartfelt poetry, offered a generous helping of sexually explicit and verbally abusive pieces. This particular phrase refers to a *sopio,* which was a caricature of a person with a rather enormous penis, something the Romans were wont to draw on walls and elsewhere, as one can tell from the quote.

aquarii

[aq-*we*-ri-ee]

water carriers

Any astrological guide today would say that an *aquarius* is inventive, bold, thoughtful, and enjoys mental challenges. But for the Romans, an *aquarius* was invariably one thing: disrespected. The *aquarii* were slaves responsible for carrying pitchers of water through the city, scattered through its dusty, noisy, chaotic streets like so many foul-mouthed water nymphs. The name literally means "of / made of water," and countless

Woman carrying water to wash a child. 3rd century CE Roman mosaic, from House of Theseus, Paphos, Cyprus.

words we use today are derived from it, including *aquarium* and *aquatic*. The *aquarii* supplied water to private homes as well as to the public baths, temples, and the many other places that needed their daily quota of water.

The *aquarii*, despite their essential role as the veins of the city, were regarded as the very lowest of the low, and were mocked and reviled by all—the satirist Juvenal tells us that these *aquarii* who hauled water up the steps of the *insulae* became the source of jokes about affairs with lonely women.

vigiles urbani
[*wi*-gi-lays ur-*ban*-ee]
city watchmen

These people were the eyes, ears, and fists of ancient Rome, in charge of firefighting and policing, patrolling through the streets night and day. Initially this started out as one gang of slaves called the *Triumviri Nocturni,* who were privately owned by a wealthy Roman citizen (although it is not known who). When complications arose, as one might expect from having a hired band of thugs in charge of the safety of the city, the emperor Augustus set up a new state force made up of 7,000 freedmen. They lived in barracks in the suburbs and navigated the city with buckets of water, pumps, axes, and hooks, ever watchful for *ignis*, "fire," and *fures*, "burglars." They were also known as *spartoli*, "bucket men," on account of the buckets they carried with them around the city. Their legacy remains in the name, for local police forces in Italy today are called the *Vigili*

Urbani, and such words as "vigilant," "vigilantes," "urban," and "urbane" derive from them.

fures
[*fou*-rays]
thieves

Ancient Rome was a notoriously dangerous place and thieves of all types ruled the streets, especially at night when the labyrinthine channels were plunged into deepest darkness. Bars were put on doors, and people sought the relative safety of their homes as night fell; Juvenal commented that leaving the house at night without making a will was just careless. In his third Satire, he wrote: *possis ignavus haberi et subiti casus inprovidus, ad cenam si intestatus eas*, "you may well be deemed a fool, improvident of sudden accident, if you go out to dinner without having made your will."

itinera
[it-in-*er*-uh]
tracks

The *itinera* were streets that only accommodated people on foot, existing from before the city had grown in size and power. They interlaced the city like capillaries, allowing passage through its seemingly impenetrable clots of buildings. From here we get the words "itinerary" and "itinerant."

in digito clavus
[in *dig*-i-toh *kla*-wus]
nail in (my) toe

Two familiar words make up this description of physical discomfort—*digitus* is the Latin word for a finger or a toe, giving us the words "digit" and "digital," and *clavus* is the Latin for a "nail" (interestingly the word "clove" derives from this word, apparently because of the shape of the plant).

One of the most distinctive sounds that echoed in ancient Rome was the clatter of soldiers' boots as they marched through the streets. Their boots were a bit like sandals, *caliga*, but with nails fitted in the soles, which enabled them to march long distances over difficult terrain. With the phrase quoted above, Juvenal described how, in the mayhem of one particular street, the hobnail of a soldier's boot had stuck painfully into his toe.

Roman soldiers from a Roman pavement mosaic, 1st–2nd century CE.

plurimus hic aeger moritur vigilando
[*plu*-rim-us hik *ey*-ger *mor*-it-ur wig-il-*an*-doh]
most sick people here die from insomnia

So Juvenal commented bitterly in his third Satire, a remark that
has since become almost proverbial about the immense noise
and clatter of the streets of Rome, day and night.

Julius Caesar banned traffic from going through the streets
during daylight hours due to the danger of adding vehicles and
beasts of burden to the already overflowing narrow streets. As
a result, as twilight deepened into darkness, the rickety clatter
of the wagons and carts making their way back through the city
replaced the shouts and grinds of the daytime. So the Romans
who were not wealthy enough to position their houses in the
more prestigious parts of the city, or who did not have the means
to build thick walls to keep out the noise, faced the burden of
noisy streets all day and night, and the frustrating lack of sleep
that accompanied this.

Graecam urbem
[*Grey*-kam *ur*-bem]
a Greek city

So Juvenal called the city of Rome, in his disdain and despair for
the influx of foreigners who had made him feel a stranger in the
city where he was born and bred. The inevitable result of Rome's
ever-expanding empire was an increasingly cosmopolitan city,
pleasing to some and threatening to others.

Juvenal bitterly referred to the Greek manners and customs that some of his compatriots were adopting as effeminate, exaggerated, and decadent, from new-fangled footwear to the diets and theatrics he cited as being peculiarly Greek.

magna taberna
[*mag*-nah tab-*ern*-ah]
one big shop

The phrase above was coined by the poet Martial to describe the streets of Rome, lined as they were with vendors of all kinds. Food supply created its own complicated networks and strata of organizations and workers who swamped the city streets all through the working day. *Vinarii*, "vintners," would travel with their goods placed into *amphorae*, large "jugs," on rickety carts; *fructarii* "fruit-sellers,"(where our word "fructose" comes from), *piscatores*, "fishmongers," and many others catered to the nutritional needs of the citizenry.

Alongside the trades that satisfied the basic requirements of the populace, providing the staple diet and necessities, purveyors of more refined and luxurious goods also thrived. Around one corner, one might have found *margaritarii*, "pearl-sellers," *violarii*, "florists," and *sagarii*, "cloak-makers"; down another narrow, twisting street were *pigmentarii*, "perfumists," and *eborarii*, "ivory-sellers."

The jostle and commotion in the streets was something recorded with exasperation by many writers. Juvenal's are the most colorful of all, with phrases such as *ego vel Prochytam praepono Suburae,* "I prefer Prochtya to Subura." Here he is referring to the Subura, which was known as one of the noisiest, grimiest streets in ancient Rome, and stating his preference for being on a distant, peaceful island. Situated between the Vimina and Esquiline hills in central Rome, the Subura seethed with hawkers, manufacturing warehouses, shops, and brothels.

quis potest sine offula vivere
[qwis pot-est si-nay off-you-ler wi-wer-eh]
who can live without a bite to eat?

The *cauponae,* "taverns," thrived on street corners, often advertizing themselves, as Juvenal remarked, with a bottle hanging from a pillar. They were considered to be venues for vice—from excessive drinking and gambling to prostitution—and to be caught in one as a respectable citizen would probably have resulted in a significant fall in one's standing.

The emperor Claudius used this phrase when discussing with the Senate the restrictions that had been placed on taverns in the city, which prevented them from selling hot water and cooked meats. In this instance Claudius was advocating that the taverns should be allowed to sell food, but the emperors had a difficult relationship with them. Taverns attracted the less desirable elements in society and it is possible that the ban was put in place because the authorities felt that providing food in these venues would encourage people to linger and sit around talking which could potentially lead to plans for revolts and sedition.

The types of people who were characterized as frequenting such places were the lowly in society, and the innkeepers were portrayed as thieves and murderers throughout Roman literature. There are even some tales of witchcraft being practiced in the taverns.

It didn't help the reputation of inns that three-quarters of the innkeepers were freedmen, so were already on a low rung in society. In fact, if anyone happened to have sex with a woman who served in an inn, this was not counted as adultery or rape, since she was regarded as beneath the law.

Girl selling grapes, mosaic pavement from Basilica Aquileia, 4th century CE.

Only one type of beverage was generally available to the weary traveler, passing tradesman, or local drunk—very alcoholic wine or *vinum*. The Romans dealt with the high alcohol content by adding hot water to the wine, and often also honey, and some spices, to create a drink known as *conditum*.

tonsor
[*ton*-sor]
hairdresser

The Roman *tonsor* was equivalent to our word "barber," a word that itself comes from the Latin for a beard, *barba*. In Roman times, a skilled professional was required to clip and shave men's beards, since the tools of the trade were far less delicate and precise than those on sale today. The shop of the *tonsor* became a hub of gossip and idle chatter, as men would meet there to get their beards clipped and hear all the latest rumors flying around the city.

collegia
[col-*leg*-i-uh]
guilds

From this Latin word we derive "college" and "colleague." The guilds were a great source of suspicion for the rulers of the city. Often meeting in taverns, they represented groups as diverse as shoemakers and clothes-dyers. Inevitably, they were accused of conspiracies and rebellion, so the emperors took various measures to try to curtail them, and they were placed under state control.

nonariae
[non-*ah*-ri-ey]
women of the ninth hour

This was one of many names granted to Roman women who earned a living as prostitutes, so-called because they were prohibited from offering their services before the ninth hour of the day, when their presence on the streets would not restrict the daily work and bustle of the city. Their crepuscular existence led many to perceive them as being part human and part animal, hence the term *lupae*, "she-wolves," by which they were also known, and with their workplace often called the *lupanar*, "wolf-house."

Women of the street sometimes masqueraded in the guise of a more acceptable trade, ranging from *citharistriae*, "lyre players," and *cymbalistriae*, "cymbal players," to *ambubiae*, "dancing girls," and *mimae*, "mimes." Prostitutes were considered very low on the social strata, and sadly were often no more than children forced into the profession.

Dancer with a tambourine, from a mosaic in the house of Dionysos, 3rd century CE. Prostitutes often masqueraded as dancers and musicians.

thermae

[*turm*-ey]

public baths

Thermae were the public baths of ancient Rome, from the ancient Greek *thermos* meaning "hot," and giving us the words "thermal" and "thermometer."

Everyone in Rome would have attended the public baths— it was one of the only equalizing elements of society, and an absolutely central part of Roman daily life.

On entering the baths, after paying a small fee, people would take off all their clothes and wear only sandals to protect their feet from the heated floors. A common way of spending

Section of mosaic floor depicting a seahorse. A mosaic from the Roman Baths at Bath, UK.

time there would have been with a workout in the *palaestra,* "gym," perhaps a ball game or two, followed by plunging into a *frigidarium,* "cold bath." Visitors would then swiftly enter the *tepidarium,* which was lukewarm, and finally the *caldarium,* which was the hot bath, and gives us the word "cauldron."

forica
[*for*-i-kah]
public toilets

Lacking our modern taboos concerning ablution, the Romans were quite happy to perform these acts in public, and the intricate and ornate decorations on the public latrines divulge their very different attitudes to the necessities of the human body. The latrines were situated in a semicircle, and the individual seats were made of marble, and decorated with all manner of images such as dolphins, gods, and heroes.

The *forica* were used by the more well-to-do in society. Lower down the rung, people would use a series of jars arranged outside the fuller's workshop, who then used the urine collected for his cleaning and dyeing trade.

Alternatively, people would use personal pots, that they would bring to the street, and tip into a *lacus* or "cesspit." This was a vile-smelling, deadly place; for this reason, unwanted children were often left here, as it was highly likely that they would die quickly from all the foul bacteria that resided in the trenches.

sterculinum publicum!

[*ster*-kyou-*lin*-um *poub*-lik-um]

you public toilet!

This charming expression comes down to us courtesy of the Roman playwright Plautus. Playwrights were a great source of insults, since they were more likely to use colloquialisms and lowbrow expressions in their works than poets or other writers. Some other common terms of abuse were *stercoreus*, "smelling of shit," and *spurcifer*, "filth-carrier."

cucurbita!

[ku-*kurb*-it-uh]

pumpkin!

Anyone familiar with planting vegetables and fruit will recognize the *cucurbita* as a family of fruit including the squash and pumpkin. The word comes from the Latin word for a pumpkin, but the Romans had a rather different colloquial use for the word as an insult to their friends, relatives, and enemies. In fact, use of the plant world as a verbal weapon against fellow human beings was quite a common form of abuse—for example, *fungi* was an insult directed at groups of people, translated as "you mushrooms!"

pauper
[*paw*-per]
beggar

Begging was a central feature on the streets of ancient Rome. Around every corner of the boisterous, bartering world of the city were people asking for money or handouts. While the majority of the inhabitants of Rome were poor, those who begged were perceived as particularly on the margins of society.

The streets were harsh and unforgiving for beggars. They were feared and avoided because of their physical appearance, the threat of contagion from any illnesses they may have had, and also because of the notion that there might be some kind of metaphysical contagion, i.e. that one might catch some kind of bad luck from them. The Roman author Seneca described how people would throw alms to beggars from a distance.

venenum
[wen-*nay*-num]
a drink of the goddess Venus

Originating from the name of the Roman goddess of love, Venus, this word had several meanings, ranging from love potions and charms to remedies and poisons. It comes into English as the word "venom." In ancient Rome, as in other cities of the time, there were purveyors of drugs to cure, to coax, and to kill, and there are many references to people hawking, buying, and using drugs. Martial, renowned for his crude and sexually explicit epigrams, commented that a man who "can't get it up" has tried all manner of *bulbique salaces*, "worts and bulbs," to solve his problem. A wide variety of plants, ointments, and potions were imported to Rome from Egypt, Spain, and other regions to satisfy the public's desire for pleasure. These would be stored in *apothecae*, "storerooms," and sold in certain quarters of the city.

acetabularii
[a-ke-tab-oul-*ah*-ri-ee]
vinegar cups

An *acetabular* now refers to a certain type of cup-shaped joint, the socket of the hip bone, into which the head of the femur fits. The *acetabularii* were the name of street magicians in ancient Rome who used a magic trick involving stones and vinegar cups to entertain and astonish the crowds. The trick they performed was called *acetabula et calculi*, "cups and balls," and much like the modern version of this familiar trick, the magicians would make it appear as if the stones had magically moved from one cup to another, or passed through the solid bottoms of the cups.

As well as magicians, street performers such as *pilarii*, "jugglers," and *ventilatores*, "knife-throwers," were known to haunt the city and entertain crowds with their acts. While musicians played for money, a law of the Twelve Tables stated that singing songs in public that parodied the government in any way was punishable by death.

ad casum tabulae
[ad *cas*-um *tab*-oo-ley]
to the hazards of the (gambling) table

This is plucked from a lengthy rant of Juvenal on the madness of gambling, something the Romans became increasingly keen on. *Casum* means a "disaster" or, at least, an unexpected event that was bad, and gives us our word "casualty." Gambling became so widespread that the authorities placed harsh penalties on anyone caught gambling outside of the "Saturnalia"

Dice players, 3rd century CE Roman mosaic, from El-Jem, Tunisia, North Africa.

festival, with the exception of bets placed on physical activities. As a result the *circuses* raked in the bets. The restrictions had a limited impact, so that Juvenal could refer to the general Roman love of gambling as *simplex furor*, "a simple form of madness."

non scholae sed vitae discimus
[nohn *sko*-ley sed *wi*-tey dis-*ki*-mus]
We learn not for school, but for life

Seneca, a Roman philosopher, said these words in a letter as a warning to avoid drifting too far into the lofty heights of philosophical debate. School was a part of daily life for boys from reasonably wealthy families, and was based around learning by rote; failure to memorize the lesson often resulted in a beating. The schools were not usually buildings in their own rights, but rather the back part of shops, separated from the street crowds only by a curtain.

Children would write on wax tablets, which they scratched their numbers and letters into, or *papyri*, using ink. They went to school seven days a week and school started before sunrise, though they did have a lot of holidays, including market days and religious festivals.

defixiones
[de-fiks-i-*oh*-nays]
curse scrolls

Romans were deeply superstitious and, without much hope of social mobility, the belief and practice of magic and witchcraft was particularly strong. It acted as a means of fantasizing about things outside of their grasp—wealth, comfort, women, revenge, justice. A common method the Romans used to get what seemed unattainable was to create a curse scroll, or *defixione*, from the verb *defigo* meaning "I bind." To make one of these, one selected a god or goddess to pray to (favorites were the underworld gods such as Hecate), then wrote what one wanted to happen to a particular person, and why, then rolled it up and nailed it to the home of the person you wanted revenge against. These were immensely popular and fragments of such scrolls have been found all over the Roman world.

amuletum
[am-oo-*let*-um]
amulet

The Roman author Pliny wrote about the importance of amulets in ancient Rome, which were used as protection against evil and misfortune. Amulets varied in form; they could be stones, plants, or even scraps of writing. They were usually tied to a part of the body, and used to protect, heal, and keep a person safe from all manner of dangers and troubling aspects of life.

Customs such as this give us an idea of the level of superstition that pervaded Roman society, alongside the officially sanctioned forms of superstition that were part of the state religion. All kinds of strange beliefs seem to have haunted the Romans in their daily lives as omens of bad luck to come—meeting a mule on the street who happened to be carrying the wrong sort of herb, spilling water, falling snakes . . . the list goes on. A particular example was a cock crowing just before a meal. This was seen as an interruption of the ceremony of the meal, and in such cases it was believed to be bad luck to eat, even if it was an important or lavish banquet that had been in preparation for days. Either someone had to cast the correct spell to combat the omen, or nothing would be eaten for the rest of the day.

sagae
[*sa*-gey]
witches

Witches were one of the many superstitions that permeated ancient Roman life, and many a conversation on a street corner or in a local tavern might involve passing on stories about a local witches' coven. The word comes from the Latin *sagire*, meaning "to predict," this gives us our word "sage," meaning both wise and a wise person.

The Roman novelist Apuleius is the most well-known teller of such tales with his story about the Thessalian witches who gnawed people's faces off, but other authors such as Horace also spread similar stories and fears abroad. He told the tale of a witch called Canidia, who stole a Roman boy and buried him up to his chin in order to remove his liver and use it in a love potion. Children were often regaled with witch tales, as Roman mothers were known to scare their children with stories of a witch-like, child-eating, and generally unpleasant character known as the Lamia.

Witches or sorcerers, providing a magical consultation. 1st century CE mosaic from Pompeii, Italy.

carpe diem
"pluck the day"
per ardua ad astra
"through difficulties to the stars"

RES GENERALIS

"general things"

Many of the words and phrases from ancient Roman culture have reached us inside our own language, through centuries of shifting and morphing, and we use them every day without realizing their Latin ancestry and origin.

An obvious example is the use of "etc," which, in its extended form *et cetera*, means "and the rest," and has become a way of saying "I could go on . . .," "there's too much to mention," or, in some cases, "I've actually run out of things to say, but want to pretend I haven't."

And if our daily conversations are littered with these examples, there are even more to be found in specialist areas, where using a Latin phrase to express something can be more succinct, or simply sound grander. Whatever the reason, one hears numerous different Latin phrases in all walks of life, so here are some of them.

a priori

[a pri-*or*-i]

from what was before

Commonly used in a legal sense this denotes something known previously, and also, in the arena of logic, to describe something which is obvious or self-evident.

ad absurdum

[ad ab-*sur*-dum]

to the point of absurdity

A shortened version of *reductio ad absurdum*, which means "reduced to the point of absurdity," and is used in the context of argument, where one takes a claim to its most extreme and ridiculous conclusion in an attempt to prove the claim itself to be false.

ad hominem

[ad *hom*-in-em]

appealing to feelings rather than reason

The phrase literally means "to the man," and includes any argument that involves an element of hysteria, emotional ranting, blackmail, manipulation, and very little in the way of logic or rationality.

ad nauseam

[ad *naw*-se-am]

to sickness

Meaning "to a ridiculous/nauseating degree," this is often used to refer to arguments where someone just repeats themselves, but it can be applied to pretty much any area of life where someone or something is doing something over and over again.

alea iacta est
[*al*-e-uh *yak*-tuh est]
the die has been cast
The Roman historian Suetonius quotes Julius Caesar as saying this in 49 BCE when he crossed the Rubicon (although Caesar actually stole the phrase from ancient Greek comedy). Crossing the Rubicon was a definitive act of defiance and the beginning of the civil war against Pompey and the Optimates; the phrase has since come to mean a decision that is a "point of no return."

alma mater
[*al*-muh *ma*-tur]
nourishing mother
A description in ancient Rome of the mother goddess, this has come to be used in contemporary English to refer to one's school or college, even if nourishment was not quite the experience one remembers from those days.

bona fide
[*bon*-ah *fi*-day]
in good faith
This phrase is commonly used in English to describe something that is genuine, usually an agreement, offer, or intention of some kind.

carpe diem
[*car*-pey *di*-em]
pluck the day

This is without doubt one of the most famous of all Latin phrases, courtesy of the Roman poet Horace's *Odes*. Although it is often translated rather more loosely as "seize the day," it literally means "pluck the day," as one might pick a flower, and refers to the sentiment that we should live our lives to the full and savor every second.

cui bono?
[*koo*-i *bon*-oh]
good for whom?

The Roman author Cicero attributes this to a censor and consul, L. Cassius. It is used to imply that the motives of a person or organization should be scrutinized to see who might benefit from a given course of action, usually a crime.

cum grano salis
[cum *gra*-noh *sal*-is]
with a grain of salt

The Roman author Pliny the Elder coined this famous phrase, when writing about an antidote for poison, which was, as you may have guessed, a grain of salt. So to take something with a grain of salt came to mean to take it in a less serious way.

deus ex machina
[*day*-us ex mah-*keen*-uh]
god out of the machine

This originally comes from tragic plays in ancient Greece, where sometimes at the end of a play, a deity was lowered onto the stage using a crane, and would resolve the crisis in the play.

divide et impera
[di-*vi*-deh et *im*-per-uh]
divide and rule
This has become a popular expression since Julius Caesar used it, and is employed in all kinds of arenas of life, often expressed as "divide and conquer."

emeritus
[e-*mer*-i-tus]
having earned discharge through service
This word is used to describe someone of importance in a given profession who has retired; this means that they can continue to use their professional title by affixing this word to it, which is useful in all kinds of ways, notably when delivering speeches or writing papers.

ex cathedra
[ex ca-*tay*-druh]
from the chair
A phrase from Catholic theology which means a teaching made by the Pope that is infallible by virtue of the Pope's position. The *cathedra* is the mark of a teacher in the ancient world, and has come to refer to the office of a person in the church.

fac simile
[fak *sim*-i-leh]
make something similar
This is where our word "facsimile" and hence "fax machine" comes from, for the obvious reason that a fax machine makes something similar.

hic sunt dracones
[hik sunt dra-*coh*-nays]
here there are dragons
Cartographers write these words on unknown areas of maps, in much the same way as mythical creatures used to be drawn onto these unexplored areas in medieval times. Apparently computer coders have been known to use the phrase to identify peculiar bits of code that should be left well alone . . .

ibidem
[*ib*-id-em]
in the same place
You often find this word abbreviated to *ibid* in the footnotes of books, and it means that the quote used came from the same source as the quote used immediately before in the text.

in loco parentis
[in *lo*-koh pa-*ren*-tis]
in place of a parent
Organizations such as schools, and in previous times, universities, held certain legal responsibilities akin to parental ones for the minors in their care.

in medias res
[in *med*-i-as race]
into the middle of things
Horace coined this phrase in his work on literary criticism, the *Ars Poetica* ("Art of Poetry"); it refers to the narrative technique of beginning a poem part way through the story line.

ipso facto
[*ip*-soh *fac*-toh]
by that very fact
This seems to crop up in all arenas of life, from colloquial usage, to legal, philosophical, and artistic. It means an effect that happens precisely because of a specific action.

lex talionis
[leks tal-i-*oh*-nis]
law of retaliation
An ancient legal concept that traces back to the Bible and beyond, this means essentially "an eye for an eye," and is based around a system of revenge and retribution for crimes.

magnum opus
[*mag*-num *o*-pus]
great work
This term refers to an artist's most renowned creation, a masterpiece.

malum discordiae
[*mah*-lum dis-*kord*-i-aye]
apple of discord

The famous apple of classical myth, which was sent from the goddess Eris (meaning "Strife"), and caused so much trouble, in fact started the Trojan War. In Latin *malum* can mean both "apple" and "evil," so in fact the expression also contains a pun.

mea culpa
[*may*-uh *cul*-puh]
my fault

This phrase originates from a prayer in the Roman Catholic mass known as the *confiteor*, which itself means "I confess," and it has come in common parlance to be a slightly pretentious way of saying "Okay, that was my fault. Sorry."

memento mori
[me-*men*-toh *mor*-i]
remember to die

Said to be used in ancient Rome when a triumphant general was paraded through the streets, its meaning is simply that one who was victorious should remember that all such things can be toppled in a day, for he is only mortal. It's a slightly more depressing spin on the phrase *carpe diem*.

mutatis mutandis
[moo-*tah*-tees moo-*tan*-dees]
the necessary changes being made

A term from law and economics to denote that changes have

been made to a previous document, it literally means "with those things having been changed which need to be changed."

non sequitur
[non *sek*-it-ur]
it does not follow

A favorite of people who think they're a dab hand at logic, this means that the conclusion does not follow logically from its premise. It's also used to describe a technique of humor, where exactly the same thing happens but to comedic effect.

o tempora o mores!
[oh *temp*-or-uh oh *mor*-ays]
oh the times oh the morals!

This lament comes from the Roman author Cicero, who observed the darker side of human nature and society and often detailed the vices of mankind in his speeches.

per ardua ad astra
[per *ahr*-doo-uh ad *ast*-ruh]
through difficulties to the stars

The motto of the Royal Air Force, and various other air forces, its heritage and meaning are both subject to debate. A similar version, *per aspera ad astra*, "through hardships to the stars," is used by NASA.

per capita
[per *cap*-it-uh]
by the head

A term used in statistics to give an average per person of things like income and crime. It's also used in wills to state that each beneficiary should receive an equally divided amount.

per centum
[per-*sent*-um]
by the hundred

An almost universally familiar expression, it expresses the proportion of a particular thing in relation to the whole, usually the amount per one hundred.

persona non grata
[per-*soh*-nuh nohn *grah*-tuh]
an unwelcome person

Associated with diplomatic relations, this labels someone, a diplomat from a particular country, for example, as being not welcome. It is sometimes used colloquially to describe someone who is considered to have stepped out of line in a given community or arena.

pro bono
[proh *bon*-oh]
on behalf of the good

A shortened form of *pro bono publico,* "for the public good," this refers to work that is done without charge in the public interest.

quid pro quo
[kwid proh kwoh]
something for something
A quicker, simpler, and fancier way of saying "you scratch my back, I'll scratch yours," these three words express the ancient and perpetually relevant code of conduct whereby someone will do a favor in exchange for some favor in return.

quo vadis?
[kwoh *vah*-dis]
where are you going?
Taken from John's gospel, where it can be found in the Greek, and is used when someone is going away on a long journey. It's since become the title of a nineteenth-century novel, several films, a song, and even a German board game.

quod erat demonstrandum (abbreviated QED)
[kwod *e*-rat de-mon-*stran*-dum]
that which was to be proved
A translation into Latin of an expression in the Greek used by the mathematicians Euclid and Archimedes, it is written (as an abbreviation) at the end of a mathematical proof or philosophical argument, showing that the last statement was in fact the proof.

sic transit gloria mundi
[sik *trans*-it *glor*-i-uh *mun*-di]
thus passes the glory of the world
This is generally taken to mean that grandeur and glory are

transient, and that humans are only mortal; it is said by a monk at papal coronations, apparently to remind the pope that he is just a man.

sine qua non
[*seen*-ay kwah non]
without which not
First found in the works of Aristotle, this has since passed into legal terminology to refer to an indispensable condition.

sub rosa
[sub *ro*-sah]
under the rose
This phrase, popularized in the medieval practice of hanging a rose from the ceiling of a court, originates from classical mythology, where Venus, the goddess of love, gave a rose to her son, Cupid. He then passed the rose to the god of silence, Harpocrates, to ensure that the gods' various indiscretions were kept secret.

tempus fugit
[*temp*-us *foo*-git]
time flees
Commonly mistranslated as "time flies," this comes from the *Georgics*, a poem written by Virgil.

terra firma
[*ter*-ruh *firm*-uh]
firm land
This expression is used to signify dry land, as opposed to sea, and was used in Venice, for example, to refer to the mainland areas of the region.

veni, vidi, vici
[*vay*-nee *vee*-dee *vee*-chi]
I came, I saw, I conquered
Julius Caesar sent this self-confident little message to the Roman Senate after his battle against King Pharnaces II in 47 BCE. Three years later, he was assassinated.

vice versa
[vice *ver*-suh]
with position having been turned
A hugely common phrase, this means the order of something being reversed.

Roman poets and writers featured in the book

Titus Maccius Plautus (Plautus) ca. 254 – 184 BCE

A Roman playwright whose works were some of the earliest we have from Roman literature. He was also a pioneer of musical theater, and works influenced or inspired by Plautus are often called "Plautine."

Marcus Pacuvius (Pacuvius) ca. 220 – 130 BCE

A great tragic poet, and a pupil (as well as nephew) of the famous epic poet Ennius. We have only fragments of his dramas left today; he was also known to be a painter.

Gaius Lucilius (Gaius Lucilius) ca. 180 – 103 BCE

The earliest Roman satirist we know of; only fragments remain of his works today.

Marcus Tullius Cicero (Cicero) 106 – 43 BCE

A very famous Roman statesman, orator, lawyer, and philosopher, Cicero is best-known as a speaker and prose writer, and admired for his many speeches, works, and letters.

Publius Vergilius Maro (Virgil) 70 – 19 BCE

A poet who composed the *Eclogues*, the *Georgics*, and finally the *Aeneid*, the patriotic epic which told of the legendary founding of Rome.

Quintus Horatius Flaccus (Horace) 65–8 BCE

A lyric poet who composed his *Odes*, *Epodes,* and *Satires*, amongst other things and is particularly well known for coining phrases such as *carpe diem*.

Publius Ovidius Naso (Ovid) 43 BCE – 17 CE

A poet who wrote the *Amores, Heroides, Ars Amatoria, Metamorphoses,* and *Fasti*, who was exiled by the emperor Augustus, and then wrote the *Tristia* and *Ex Ponto* from exile.

Titus Petronius (Petronius) ca. 27 – 66 CE

A well-known Roman satirist of Nero's time, his most famous work was thought to have been the *Satyricon*, a comic satirical novel about the adventures of two men. According to Roman historian Tacitus, he was said to have been a courtier of Nero's named Petronius, but this identification is uncertain.

Gaius or Caius Plinius Caecilius (Pliny) ca. 61–113 CE

A writer and lawyer, who wrote many letters, and who famously witnessed the eruption of Vesuvius in 79 CE.

Gaius Suetonius Tranquillus (Suetonius) ca. 69/75 – after 130 CE

A biographer and historian, and a close friend of Pliny the Younger. He is best known for his work *About the Lives of the Twelve Caesars*, a biography of the Roman Empire's first leaders.

Decimus Iunius Iuvenalis (Juvenal) unknown

A poet who was alive in the late 1st century/early 2nd century CE, and who wrote the Satires.

Marcus Valerius Martialis (Martial) unknown

A poet, he wrote epigrams published in Rome between 86 and 103 CE. His poems were usually witty, satirical, and often very rude.

PRONUNCIATION GUIDE

The words in this book are shown as phonetically pronounced by an English speaker, with the stress shown in italics. Where some compound words, as in German, have two stresses, the first will be the stronger. Some specific vowels and consonants are indicated below.

j – is the French sound j –, a soft, slurred jay.
dj – is the English sound j – in jail.
tch – is the sound ch – in chatter.
ch – or – ch is the sound – ch in Scottish loch.
– onh is the nasal French sound on.
– anh is the nasal French sound in.
– o – is a short – o – as in hot.
– oh – is a long – o – as in comb.
– a – is a short – a – as in fat.
– ay – is the long – a – as in fake.
– ah is a long – a – as in far.
– i is a short – i – as in dip.
– ey – is a long – i – as in hide.
– er is the sound – e in the.
– eh is the short – e – as in let
(used where there is no following consonant).
– u – is a short – u – as in put.

Phonetics in chapter 5 are for modern pronunciations.

ACKNOWLEDGMENTS

There are so many people in my life who have offered support, insights, ideas, and inspiration along the way, that listing them would be a book in itself! If I were being forced, by a crotchety Roman emperor for example, to single people out from so many, I would choose my school Latin teacher Mr. Northwood, who opened my eyes to such a fascinating world of language and culture, my two classes at Benthal primary school in Hackney that provided me with many hours of endlessly entertaining Latin lessons, and John Kimbell, governor at the school, without whom those hours would never have happened.

Finally, I would want to thank my friends and family for putting up with me while I was writing this book!

Picture Credits:
Art Archive: pp. 2, 10, 14, 17, 21, 32, 35, 38, 41, 51, 56, 61, 63, 67, 70, 75, 78, 82, 86, 89, 93, 95, 101, 105, 106, 128
Dreamstime: p. 45
Drazen Tomic: Endpapers, map of Rome (from *Ancient Rome on Five Denarii a Day* by Philip Matyszak, Thames & Hudson Ltd., London)

WORD FINDER

A

B

C

D

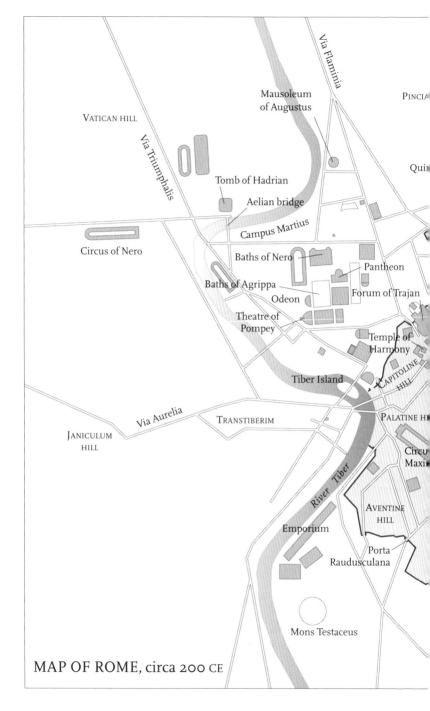

MAP OF ROME, circa 200 CE